The Naked Truth...

about Publishers Clearing House

The Naked Truth about
Publishers Clearing House

Darrell Lester

PENNYWYSE
PRESS
TUCSON, ARIZONA

Published in the United States of America by:

Pennywyse Press
3710 East Edison Street
Tucson, AZ 85716

Library of Congress Control Number: 2011918168

ISBN 978-1-935437-42-0
ISBN 1-935437-42-9

Book and Cover Design by Leila Joiner
Cover photograph by Alex Amoling and Lowell Meyer

Printed in the United States of America on Acid-Free Paper

Table of Contents

INTRODUCTION 7

CHAPTER

1 The Question Everyone Asks 13

2 The Beginning 18

3 PCH Winner Stories – Part 1 31

4 My Early Days 47

5 They Loved Us 62

6 The Key to Our Incredible Success – Testing, Testing, Testing . .73

7 My Big Decision 80

8 The First PCH Scandal – Arnold Diaz 84

9 The Roller Coaster Ride Up – The Good Times at PCH 88

10 The Firestorm of Negative Press 101

11 The Legal Troubles for PCH – It's Raining Lawsuits 109

12 The Roller Coaster Ride Down – The Bad Times at PCH 124

13 The Penalty Doesn't Fit The Crime 132

14 The Worst Three Hours of My Life 136

15 White Powder – A Second Nightmare 142

16 The Great PCH Talent 145

17 PCH Winner Stories – Part 2 154

18 The Fun We Had – Some Personal Stories 164

19 The PCH Bonus 182

20 The Best Practical Jokes and Pranks at PCH 186

21 An Apparent Suicide by One of Our Own 197

22 My Final Chapter at PCH 199

23 Life in Retirement 205

Introduction

I am going to make a very bold statement, and I guarantee that once you read the ensuing story, you will agree with my audacious declaration. *Publishers Clearing House was the most loved company in U.S. history. And also the most hated.*

I started working at PCH as a young, eager, utterly naïve twenty-one year old kid just out of college. I'd never even heard of Publishers Clearing House at the time and had no idea what I was in for. But I was about to embark on the journey of a lifetime. I ended up working at PCH for thirty years and became an integral player in virtually all of the company's major decisions and activities, for better or for worse. I was Vice President of Marketing during our enormously successful years, and my final role was as Senior Vice President. I was also one of a handful of officers of the company before retiring at a relatively young age. I didn't always agree with senior management but was known for my honesty, integrity, and objectivity – and that's how I have presented this account, including the positive and negative sides of PCH.

I lived through both "the love" and "the hate" firsthand, as well as extraordinary growth, the sudden devastating downslide, and the resulting intense battle to survive. The story of Publishers Clearing House has never been told before, and I am sure you will find it to be a captivating and fun-filled tale.

The Founding Mertz Family

PCH began as a small mom-and-pop business in the basement of the founding father's home but it quickly outgrew its home-based operation.

Although Harold Mertz had great plans for his small company, he never imagined it would become one of the most profitable private companies in America… not even in his wildest dreams.

Fortunately, Mr. Mertz was astute enough to hire an incredibly talented management team when the business started to grow, and it was these eccentric and playful executives that made *Publishers Clearing House* a household name and one of the top five most recognizable companies in the country.

It is also noteworthy that amidst PCH's spectacular notoriety, good and bad, the founding Mertz family was quietly becoming one of the top twenty most philanthropic families in America – giving almost $1 billion over their lifetime. Not bad for a company started by one man in the basement of his home with his wife and daughter helping.

The Love

The love for Publishers Clearing House by the general public and the media at large can be measured by the unprecedented amount of free favorable publicity directed at PCH, the popular Prize Patrol, and our colorful contest winners. This positive publicity appeared far and wide – on television, in print, and in film – and included praiseworthy news reports, good-natured parodies, amusing jokes, fun cartoons, light-hearted interviews of our contest winners, and frequent chronicles of the legendary Prize Patrol.

There is no doubt that Publishers Clearing House is now a part of American pop culture and no denying the company's widespread renown. The list of television shows that embraced PCH is incredibly long and includes the best-of-the-best, like *Seinfeld, Cheers, Letterman, Leno, Saturday Night Live, Oprah,* and many more. In addition, there was a time when our good name was constantly in the news, including local coverage, network news, and nationally aired programs such as *Dateline NBC, 48 Hours,* and *Behind Closed Doors with Joan Lunden.* Plus, PCH and the Prize Patrol have been the subject of an unending parade of comic strips that have been enjoyed by millions of consumers around the country.

I will share some of the best parodies, jokes, and cartoons in this book. And, of course, the PCH legacy would not be complete without tales of our millionaire contest winners, their winning moments, and Prize Patrol adventures. The most memorable of these will also be shared, including the alluring account of the gorgeous eighteen-year old gal (shown on the cover) who answered her door dripping wet, wrapped only in a towel.

My personal favorite parody is an alternate ending that featured Publishers Clearing House in the final episode of *Cheers*, one of the most adored television sitcoms ever. Very few people know about this delightful other ending which was filmed but never aired. I know you'll enjoy hearing which beloved character from Boston's most famous bar was surprised by the Prize Patrol and won the big prize.

In today's world, the peak of the "PCH mania" is gone. But the legacy lingers on, as can be found in many media events just over this past year. Here are a few relevant examples.

For his new late-night show on TBS, talk show host Conan O'Brien impersonates the PCH Prize Patrol in some of his commercials.

The real Prize Patrol makes a surprise appearance on the new CBS daytime show, "*The Talk*," with hosts Sharon Osbourne and other female personalities.

Comedian Jerry Seinfeld tells a well-received joke referencing PCH at a celebrity-filled party at the Obama White House honoring Sir Paul McCartney.

These recent examples prove America still remembers Publishers Clearing House.

The Hate

At the pinnacle of PCH's success, an incident sparked by an addicted sweepstakes consumer ignited an avalanche of lawsuits and negative publicity. This turned the tides against PCH and the entire sweepstakes industry.

We were sued by virtually every one of the fifty state Attorneys General and faced dozens of additional lawsuits as well. There aren't many other companies, if any, that have been subjected to that many lawsuits. Besides Publishers Clearing House, I know of only one other industry that has been involved in this many legal disputes – the to-bacco companies – and we all know their product kills.

The PCH management team battled the Attorneys General, law-yers, and politicians for four long, damaging years. It was like we were caught in quicksand, and every time a settlement was near, we were dragged back in. What other company has negotiated a national class action settlement, approved by a federal judge, only to find the agree-ment made matters worse, bringing on even more lawsuits? This na-tionally approved settlement offered refunds to 43 million American households, the largest class action group in United States history, but to the shock of PCH management and our advisors, even that didn't satisfy the appetite of the Attorneys General and politicians. You'll hear both sides of the legal argument in the ensuing chapters.

As if the lawsuits weren't troubling enough, the news media seemed to relish showing the misery and despair of elderly consumers who were addicted to sweepstakes. The very same news reporters who had previ-ously embraced the heart-warming winning moments of our big contest winners, and who had fought to go on a Prize Patrol adventure, had no second thoughts about jumping on the bandwagon to report negative and damaging stories about PCH. One example, and there were many, was an elderly widow who was so obsessed with sweepstakes that she defiantly moved away from her family who objected to her addiction. Other distressing accounts of addicted sweepstakes consumers are doc-umented as well.

The end result of the negative publicity and countless lawsuits was inconceivable as the entire direct marketing industry, including PCH, was brought to its knees. There would, in fact, be very few survivors.

My Personal Story

This book, however, is not just the account of a remarkable one-of-a-kind company. It is also about my own personal thirty-year journey at Publishers Clearing House, starting fresh out of college all the way to my retirement. And it includes the gamut of every conceivable emotion.

On the positive side, it reveals tremendous levels of satisfaction from my dreamlike success, deep appreciation for an unexpected act of kindness from our CEO, riotous and contagious laughter resulting from senior management's mischievous pranks, and complete joy in watching my young twin daughters running up and down the PCH hallways.

On the other end of the emotional spectrum, it includes unending frustration over our legal quagmire, embarrassment from the hurtful news stories, profound sadness when one of our own apparently took his life, extreme panic at being in the midst of an anthrax scare at our Port Washington headquarters, and intense fear and rage as I sat in my office while my identical twin brother was in one of the World Trade Center's Twin Towers on that infamous day.

I considered PCH my second home and came to know everyone who worked there, from the very top level to the cleaning crew. In addition to my own experience at this captivating company, this book includes stories, memories, and revelations from dozens of former PCH employees, including secretaries, clerks, managers, directors, vice presidents, and former presidents. Some of the employees who contributed to this book worked twenty, thirty, and forty years for PCH. One colleague was even there the very first day the business started and worked for the company's founder for almost fifty years.

So sit back and enjoy the ride as you travel with me from the founding years of PCH through the ups and downs to where PCH is today.

1   The Question Everyone Asks

Before I chronicle the story of Publishers Clearing House, let me clear up some misconceptions and answer a question I am constantly asked. This particular question has been asked countless times by the media, family, friends, and acquaintances. It's the very first thing people want to know when they discover I worked for Publishers Clearing House. You know the question:

"Does PCH really award all those prizes?"

Not to keep you wondering, I'll answer this question right up front. Since PCH started using sweepstakes back in 1967, over $225 million in total prizes have been awarded and dozens of consumers across the country have been made millionaires. To be exact, as of early 2011, PCH has made over fifty individuals from all around the United States millionaires. The breakdown is as follows:

- 37 winners of $1 million
- 2 winners of $2 million
- 12 winners of $10 million
- 1 winner of $21 million
- 1 winner of $5,000 a week for life

If you average this out, PCH has made two fortunate individuals millionaires (or multi-millionaires in some cases) every year for the past twenty-five years. In addition, thousands of other prizes are given away every year, including smaller cash prizes ranging from $100 to $100,000, exotic vacations, cars, and home electronics. That is why the national media, consumers, and the direct marketing and publishing industries call Publishers Clearing House the "Granddaddy of Sweepstakes." So the answer to the question that I have been asked hundreds of times is an emphatic, "YES! PCH absolutely awards all those prizes!"

I can personally attest to this statement, as I have met many of our big prize winners. Every year the top contest winners are flown to our headquarters in New York where they are treated to a weekend in Manhattan, a tour of PCH headquarters, and an all-employee party for them in our cafeteria.

This may also be hard to believe, but those people in the television commercials are all real PCH winners too, filmed in real, live, winning moments. Really!

Now that you know PCH awards all those prizes, let me clear up a few other popular misconceptions.

"Do I have to buy a magazine to win a prize?"

The truth is that consumers who order magazines and those who do not are treated exactly equally regarding the chance of winning a sweepstakes prize. The winner selections are a result of a rigorously followed procedure of random drawings from the pool of all consumers who respond to a promotion or mailing. The process is closely monitored by an outside professional accounting firm at every step along the way and by PCH employees as well.

The procedure we use absolutely gives each entrant, whether placing an order or simply returning an entry into the sweepstakes, an equal chance of winning.

With that said, let me apologize to all those consumers who send in those endearing items, such as good luck charms, poems, prayers, pictures, and home-made cakes with their entries or orders. We enjoy receiving them, but it doesn't help your chances of winning.

The Odds

The odds of winning at PCH and the other sweepstakes companies were a deep dark secret for many years. When asked by news reporters, we never gave the odds of winning because they were quite long. Often the press would report something like, "It's more likely that you would be struck by lightning than win the big PCH prize." We hated when we heard that, but we knew it was true. When federal legislation was passed in 1999, it required that the contest odds be printed in the official rules of every sweepstakes promotion. So the odds of winning are no longer a secret.

I recently checked the odds of winning the PCH top prize, and I was stunned by what I found. The odds of winning the top PCH prize in early 2011, as stated in their promotions and on their website, are "1 in 1,215,500,000." That's 1 in 1.2 billion. I was disappointed and saddened when I saw this statistic. In my day at PCH, the odds of winning the big prize were long, but nowhere near that long. It was in the millions to one in my day, not over a billion to one as it is now. These are likely the worst odds PCH has ever had for their top prize, and I surmise that this is primarily to help them reduce their costs. Despite these long odds, however, PCH still manages to make two to three lucky people rich every year.

As to the odds of being struck by lightning, the National Safety Council estimates that these odds are about 1 in 3 million. So in reality, you *are* many times more likely to be struck by lightning than to win the PCH top prize. So although PCH makes a few individuals millionaires every year there are apparently a lot more people who are struck by lightning each year. I guess it really just depends on whether it's your time!

I recently heard a hilarious comment on the news about the odds of winning. The news report stated that it is more likely that you will be killed by a toppling vending machine than win a big sweepstakes or lottery prize. But don't let that discourage you. To make you feel a little better about your odds of winning, there was one consumer whose wife retrieved the winning PCH entry from the garbage can and mailed it in. They ended up winning the big prize that year.

Ed McMahon

Another popular misconception concerns TV celebrity Ed McMahon. Virtually everyone, including the press, consumers, prize winners, and even prospective employees, thinks that Ed McMahon worked for PCH. The truth is that Ed McMahon never worked for Publishers Clearing

House. Let me say this again… *Ed McMahon never worked for Publishers Clearing House!* Both Ed McMahon and Dick Clark were spokespersons for American Family Publishers, a major PCH competitor.

You would expect the news media to be more accurate, but to our amazement, they would get this fact wrong almost every time. We often asked the press not to repeat this misconception – but even so, they still usually reported that Ed McMahon worked for PCH! I even heard there was an article once about sweepstakes in *Time* magazine, whose parent company owned American Family Publishers, which misstated that Ed McMahon was the spokesperson for PCH and not their very own AFP.

Besides the news media, our very own prize winners often make this mistake as well. We were used to our winners saying, "Why isn't Ed McMahon delivering my prize?" And when Dave Sayer, head of the PCH Prize Patrol, awards a big cash sweepstakes prize to a Publishers Clearing House winner, it is common for a bystander to yell, "So where's Ed McMahon?"

Believe it or not, even job seekers have made this mistake. Fred Neurohr, a researcher for a local youth group, tells this story about a job interview he had with Publishers Clearing House. To break the ice with the interviewer from PCH, Fred asked, "Is Ed McMahon around a lot?" Getting no answer, he persisted. "Have you met him?" Meeting more silence, Fred tried one last time. "I bet he's a trip at the holiday party." Only then did the interviewer, after rolling his eyes in frustration, reply, "He works for the competition." Oddly enough, Fred got the job and for a short time was Manager of Research at PCH.

One of the most amusing incidents pertaining to this misconception was an interview with Ed McMahon himself when he was a guest on *The Daily Show with Jon Stewart.* Jon began his interview with Ed McMahon by asking him about his work for Publishers Clearing House. Ed responded in a very annoyed tone, "No, no, no, that's another company; that's our rival!" As Jon apologized for his faux pas, Ed gave him a taste of his own medicine and quickly shot back, "Craig, anyone can make a mistake." This clever comeback got a huge laugh.

I wish I had a good explanation for this mistaken belief. I can only guess that the names "Publishers Clearing House" and "Ed McMahon" are both just so synonymous with sweepstakes that everyone assumes that Ed McMahon and PCH are one entity. In fact, Ed McMahon and PCH are so tied together in people's minds that even when Ed McMahon passed away on June 23, 2009, one question was asked over and over again, "How will Publishers Clearing House notify their winners now?" The answer was easy, "The same as they always did since Ed McMahon never worked for PCH."

At Publishers Clearing House we got to the point where this mistake became quite irritating, especially when it came from the press or prospective employees who should have known better. We didn't feel as bad when the average consumer or potential winner made this mistake, but we certainly hoped it would never happen when we began airing our live Super Bowl commercials. Now that would have been embarrassing!

What Does the Business Community Think of Sweepstakes and Contests?

It's interesting that most business leaders will say that sweepstakes and contests are gimmicky and unprofessional. And they are, to some extent, depending on how they are promoted.

But some very well-known companies and individuals have used this promotional technique. The list includes some of the most respected financial institutions around like American Express and Citibank; some of the most valued charities like St. Jude Children's Hospital and Easter Seals; some of the most popular fast food outfits like McDonald's and Burger King; some of the largest consumer goods companies like Procter & Gamble and Johnson & Johnson; and many other large and prestigious companies in virtually every industry.

Even two very famous politicians, Bill and Hillary Clinton, have used a contest at times. A recent example is from Hillary Clinton's presidential election campaign. In order for her to pay off the balance of her campaign debt, she instituted a contest in which donors of $5.00 or more got a chance to win a day with her husband, Bill Clinton. I wonder if Monica Lewinsky was allowed to enter the contest.

With that all said, in my opinion, the answer to this question is, "Yes, sweeps and contests are gimmicky," but there is also no denying that these promotional tools are extraordinarily powerful.

2   The Beginning

The Origin of Publishers Clearing House

Publishers Clearing House was founded in 1953 by Harold Mertz, along with his wife LuEsther and their daughter Joyce. The original idea came from Mr. Mertz who was forty-nine when the initial mailing took place. At the time, college students going door-to-door were the largest source of new magazine subscriptions, other than the publishers' own very limited direct mail efforts. Mr. Mertz had been working in the magazine industry for many years, including for *Look* magazine, and he had also managed some of the groups of college students going door-to-door to drum up subscriptions. During this period, the college students worked for individual publishers and only offered a single magazine subscription as part of their sales pitch. Harold knew first-hand how arduous it was for the foot soldiers to trudge through residential neighborhoods to make a sale and also how challenging it was to manage all those youngsters.

Harold believed that offering consumers a choice of many magazines at one time, instead of just one, would increase the chances that the consumer would buy something. This approach had never been done before, and although the concept was simple, it was revolutionary at the time. The cornerstone to his offer was the guarantee that the subscriptions were offered at the lowest possible introductory prices. Plus, he thought it would be better to let the U.S. Postal Service do the work instead of leaving it to door-to-door salespeople.

The very first mailing was done from Harold and LuEsther Mertz's home on Long Island, in Port Washington, New York, where they mailed out 10,000 letters. The offer let the consumer choose from among twenty discounted magazine subscriptions, rather than just one magazine, in a single mailing. This first promotion was quite uncomplicated; it included a plain white outer envelope, a flyer inside describing the magazines with their low introductory subscription prices, a short solicitation letter, and a reply envelope. There was no stampsheet with colorful stamps to lick and stick, and of course, no sweepstakes yet. But this simple initial mailing generated 100 orders, or a 1% response rate, which was encouraging enough for the Mertzes to proceed with their new business venture.

The first few years, Mr. Mertz did everything with meticulous attention to detail. He was Creative Chief, Production Manager, President, and everything else. You name it, he did it, with LuEsther and Joyce helping him. After a few years, there was enough business that Mr. Mertz moved the company out of his basement and started hiring talent to help him and his family run the business.

To Mr. Mertz, every little detail mattered. For example, when the company was big enough to have its own small group of employees handle customer service, Mr. Mertz would anonymously call every Saturday pretending to be a customer. He wanted to see for himself how his staff was handling the phone calls. This attention to detail became an essential ingredient in PCH's success. In fact, there were four fundamental philosophies held by Harold Mertz that became the foundation for his highly successful business:

1) Meticulous attention to detail and complete reporting on everything,

2) Strong belief in testing and research,

3) Full and open discussion of all decisions, including a vigorous debate on all the pros and cons, and

4) Generosity of spirit for the environment, the community, their employees, and for those less fortunate.

In addition to the four principles mentioned above, I suppose you could say the greatest element in PCH's success was Harold Mertz's willingness to be open to new ideas, as shown by his reaction to the initial test of a sweepstakes.

The First Sweepstakes

Do you have $10.00 in your pocket? If you do, you're carrying as much cash as any top prize winner ever won in the very first PCH giveaway back in 1967. That's right, I did say, "Ten dollars!"

PCH was not the first company to employ sweepstakes. That distinction goes to the Readers Digest Association, as they were the first sweepstakes direct marketer. In 1962, a young man named Gordon Grossman was inspired to try a sweepstakes at the Digest after noticing an Oldsmobile giveaway at a local car dealer. As the story goes, at first there was resistance by Readers Digest founder DeWitt Wallace, but his hesitations vanished when he saw the powerful results.

The small PCH management team at the time noticed that Readers Digest repeated their initial sweepstakes promotion. Upon seeing this, Harold Mertz, never opposed to borrowing a good idea, decided to test the use of sweepstakes for his own business. The initial 1966 test was called "Pick Your Lucky Star" because the mailing had ten stamps in the shape of stars which were affixed to the letter inside the package. The odds of winning were 1 in 10. That's not a typo... the odds of winning were 1 in 10! And as I said, the top prize was a whopping $10.00; the smallest prize amount was 25 cents.

This first PCH test of sweepstakes, in spite of the paltry top prize, did extremely well. However, Mr. Mertz had some serious reservations. After seeing the initial favorable test result, Mr. Mertz called his senior management team together to discuss the successful result. His Executive team included Henry Cowen, Lou Kislik, John Mienik, Bert Rowley, Marvin Barckley, Alan Rabinowitz, and Mike Kaufman, many who later became legends in the industry. At this somber meeting, Mr. Mertz was having second thoughts about the prospect of attaining so many new customers and passionately lectured his team on how sweepstakes could destroy his company. His concern was that the huge increase in response due to the sweepstakes promotion would bring in poor quality customers.

At the time, PCH was small but very profitable, and Mr. Mertz didn't want to jeopardize his "cash cow." At the end of his stern lecture, Mr. Mertz said, "All in favor of doing this sweepstakes and destroying my business, raise your hand." There was only one person brave enough to raise his hand. It happened to be the youngest person in the room, John Mienik, a highly charismatic copywriter at the time.

To Mr. Mertz's credit, his style was to listen to all sides of an argument before making a decision. Mr. Mertz was hesitant but agreed to proceed cautiously with sweepstakes, and as they say, the rest is history. The introduction and development of sweepstakes at PCH was probably the single biggest factor in our meteoric growth and a key part of who PCH is even today, almost fifty years later. Although I wasn't at this initial meeting on sweepstakes, I was fortunate to have known and learned from all seven of the talented PCH executives at this meeting with Mr. Mertz. To our delight, it took many years before other marketers began to understand what PCH and Readers Digest knew about the extraordinary power of sweepstakes.

Our original top prize of $10.00 was soon changed to $5,000, and the prize was gradually increased over the years. Interestingly, state lotteries were first introduced at about the same time as the start of sweepstakes. New Hampshire was the first state to introduce a lottery in 1964; many states followed soon after.

The writer of the first PCH sweepstakes package was Henry Cowen, one of the early creative geniuses at Mr. Mertz's company. In 1975, however, after fifteen years at PCH, Mr. Cowen left to form his own creative agency called The Cowen Group where he advised numerous American companies as well as companies in Canada and Europe. The clients of The Cowen Group included many prominent names like American Express, *Time*, *Newsweek*, AARP, American Automobile Association, *TV Guide*, Exxon, Conde Nast, *Sports Illustrated*, North Shore Animal League, Bantam Books, and more. The former PCH creative guru eventually became recognized as an industry icon with sixty illustrious years in direct marketing, and he received just about every direct marketing award that can be given to an individual. Mr. Cowen also taught at universities, gave seminars, and delivered talks in Canada, Germany, Sweden, Finland, Austria, and France, as well as all over the U.S.

What Were Harold and LuEsther Mertz Really Like?

Although I never personally met Harold Mertz, many of my colleagues at PCH have shared their recollections and memories about his strong and unique personality. When asked about the successful company that he had started in his basement, the modest yet jovial Harold Mertz was known to joke, "When you start in the cellar, there's only one direction to go."

I have met LuEsther Mertz, and the first time I met her she was already in her late seventies. I was giving a presentation to the Executive Committee and I knew she was going to be there, so I had rehearsed for days because of the small but important audience. In the middle of my talk, I glanced in her direction to see if she was enjoying my speech and noticed she was quietly napping! Luckily, I had been warned before my presentation that this was likely to happen. So without missing a beat, I continued with my talk. After the meeting, Mrs. Mertz kindly told me, "I liked your speech; you have excellent grammar." I was dumbfounded by her comment and found it to be quite humorous since English is not one of my strong points. I thanked Mrs. Mertz and was just glad she seemed to like me. Years later I found out she suffered from narcolepsy.

The following colorful tales about Harold Mertz and the early days at PCH will help underscore Harold Mertz's attitude and philosophy which, as I have said, became guiding principles for the company.

The Perfectionist

Jerry Reitman recounts this story about Harold Mertz. Jerry worked at PCH for six years as Vice President of Publisher Relations before going on to hold highly regarded executive positions at two of the largest and most prestigious advertising agencies in the country, Ogilvy & Mather and Leo Burnett.

Mr. Mertz was a perfectionist in many ways and wanted to be on top of all things. In the mid-1960's, a new, larger PCH headquarters was built on an impressive 14-acre site. Harold was very proud of his new building and checked everyone's work in great detail, so much so, that at night, after the construction crews had left, he would quietly climb a ladder with the blueprints in hand. He would then check that everything was being done exactly according to plan, including the tolerances between the steel girders.

I don't recall the exact tolerances required, but one time he found the slightest variation between two steel beams. The very next morning he arrived at the construction site bright and early and said to the construction chief, "The building is out of plumb!"

The crew chief replied, with patience I am told, "Mr. Mertz, we are very careful. That can't be so."

At this point, Harold insisted they climb a ladder to the roof, and with micrometer in hand, they measured the same place Mr. Mertz had found the previous evening to be slightly off. Needless to say, the construction chief and crew never questioned him again. It was this kind of attention to detail that made PCH an enormously successful enterprise.

382 Channel Drive

Along with his meticulous attention to detail and wanting everything to be perfect, Mr. Mertz also had a superstitious side. After the construction of the Port Washington headquarters was finished, Mr. Mertz insisted that the town use the number "382" for the address of the new building, even though there were only one or two other buildings on the entire long dead-end road. He believed this was his lucky number. His business was doing so well at the current location, a small building at 382 Main Street, that Mr. Mertz wanted to use the same number for the new, larger corporate headquarters. As he could be very persuasive, the town granted his unusual request.

Mr. Mertz also wanted his employees to work in a beautiful environment. The new headquarters were built with that in mind, but for the executive offices our founding father took this philosophy to another level. The furniture, walls, and doors in the executive offices, as well as the hallways, were made from very expensive teak imported from Denmark. In fact, Mr. Mertz flew to Denmark with the architect of his new building to personally select the teak, and then he had the custom order shipped back to the States. To those of us who worked at PCH, being in a teak office was the ultimate status symbol, like having a star on the Hollywood Walk of Fame. We fondly nicknamed the executive offices, "The Teak Forest." When I was moved to an office in The Teak Forest in the latter part of my career, I knew I had made it.

When the new headquarters first opened in 1967, it had lots of empty offices and open space, but it was soon filled with many very busy people. I don't believe anyone, not even Mr. Mertz, realized at the time how large his business would eventually become. It wouldn't be long before the new spacious headquarters would become overcrowded.

The FBI Visits PCH

Another demonstration of Harold Mertz's attention to detail comes from Bert Rowley, a Dartmouth graduate and very creative individual who worked at several of the major direct marketing firms. Bert is a thirty-five year veteran of Readers Digest, PCH and American Family Publishers, and former Vice President of Creative at PCH.

This is the story of the origins of the name Robert H. Treller, the fictitious company figurehead used in all PCH correspondence. Many companies back in the 1950's used fictitious characters, like Betty Crocker and Aunt Jemima, for their national advertising. Sorry if you didn't know, but Betty Crocker and Aunt Jemima are not real people! Mr. Mertz chose the name "Robert H. Treller" from a phone book for being a non-controversial John Doe type of name. For PCH, this name was used in all of our solicitation letters for many years.

Mr. Mertz, with his usual attention to detail, was quite particular about how the Treller signature appeared. The signature of Robert H. Treller was characterized by open *e*'s and boldly crossed *t*'s to suggest honesty and trustworthiness. Letters drafted by the few PCH writers, which always ended with the Treller signature, were often returned to the writer with a command from Mr. Mertz to "Get the *e*'s and *t*'s right." In a sign of respect, head artist Ralph Feuerman named his orange and white cat Robert H. Treller, and while Ralph worked, the Treller cat was a constant companion on his art board.

Such was the fictitious Treller's renown that FBI agents, apparently thinking Treller was a real person, visited PCH one day and asked to meet him. It turns out that a candidate for a sensitive federal government job had used Mr. Treller as a reference. The FBI was shocked that their job candidate's reference was not a real person.

The Treller name was used for forty-five years by PCH in countless mailings to millions of customers. From time to time, we would get letters from customers who said they were a friend of Mr. Treller, and sometimes they would even send in cookies or a cake for him to enjoy. PCH retired the Treller persona in 1999 when some U.S. Senators at the Senate Hearings strongly objected to the fact that Mr. Treller was not real. I hope they don't go after Betty Crocker and Aunt Jemima next.

The Bulls

One of the original guiding principles under which PCH operated was never to do anything that wasn't 100% proven. With regard to Harold Mertz's attitude about testing, Bob McGoff, a fun-loving, always smiling, twenty-five year veteran of PCH and former Facilities Manager, has this story to relate.

Mr. Mertz displayed a large collection of various sized statues of bulls on a large shelf behind his desk. When asked their significance, he would say, "To remind me that I am surrounded by bull shit." His employees and management team came to know never to give Mr. Mertz an answer from the hip. You had to be absolutely certain before answering him or at least have the data to back up your answer.

In the direct marketing field, unlike most industries, you can test to see the exact value of your various promotional efforts. In those early days there was one customer mailing a month, and nothing in the promotion was changed unless it was tested first. We wouldn't change a single word of the copy, nor a color, or anything else, unless it tested favorably. This philosophy, over time, resulted in an enormous testing and research program at PCH, the envy of hundreds of direct marketing companies.

The Ducks

This story, which illustrates the Mertz kindness, comes from Tom Bass, a thirty-eight year PCH veteran and former Senior Director of Purchasing and Production. I must say of Tom, he is known for his extraordinary expertise, and he is also the most trustworthy and loyal man you could ever meet.

The new PCH headquarters (shown below) included a very beautiful and large man-made pond in front of the building. Inside the large pond were three man-made islands, each with gorgeous Weeping Willow trees and low growing Juniper bushes as ground cover. Aside from the comings and goings of the employees driving around the pond, the scene was very tranquil. Naturally, it didn't take long for some ducks to realize this was an ideal location to make their nests.

PCH headquarters (Photo by Lisa)

Soon the ducks began raising their families in this idyllic location. When the numerous baby ducks first appeared, however, it became apparent that there was a major problem. The baby ducklings, once off the islands and in the water, had great difficulty getting back up onto the islands because the land was a foot higher than the water level. Upon learning this, Mr. Mertz immediately summoned the Maintenance department to build wooden ramps leading out of the water up to the level of the islands to allow the baby ducks easy access to their new habitat. In later years, concrete "steps" were cast and used like stepping stones for the ducks to access the islands.

While the ducks enjoyed a seemingly perfect setting, especially with their new access ramps, all was still not good. Sometimes the local teenagers would come by with their BB guns to shoot at the ducks. The adult ducks would quickly take refuge in the bushes, but the babies didn't have as much sense… and there were some casualties. One May, just after the babies hatched, there was concern over the fate of the cute, little critters during the upcoming three day Memorial Day weekend. There would be no one around over the long holiday weekend, and the local juvenile hunters would have free reign. In response to this dire situation, PCH paid one of our warehouse workers along with his wife to sit and guard the pond each day throughout the Memorial Day weekend. John and Diane Boeren sat peacefully with beach chairs and umbrellas watching over the pond, reading and sipping their favorite beverages. Needless to say, the baby ducks were safe.

The Generosity of the Mertzes

Starting in the 1960's, over 40% of PCH profits went to charities, the arts, and social causes. To the credit of the PCH owners, they never sought recognition for their philanthropic endeavors.

I recall at one point we discussed whether we should take advantage of the owners philanthropic activities in our promotions. One of our new competitors in the 1980's, Great American Magazines, tried to differentiate themselves from the big guys (PCH and AFP) by promoting the fact that they would donate $1.00 to charity for every magazine subscription. This new competitor was founded by Avon, the cosmetics giant, and they promoted themselves as "The sweepstakes company with a heart." At PCH, we discussed the possibility of touting the Mertz family contributions, but this wasn't something our founders wanted to do. They said, "The full thanks we get is our ability to do it, and not in thanks back." And they actually meant it.

I estimate that over their lifetime and up through 2011, the Mertz family has given about $780 million to charities, social causes, and the arts. There are only a handful of individuals, families, or companies that have ever been so generous.

A recent survey by *BusinessWeek* listed the top fifty most generous philanthropists in the United States. The Mertz family wasn't on this list, probably because they never sought the spotlight. But if they had been included, the Mertz family would have ranked in the top twenty – behind some of the most recognizable names in the United States, like Warren Buffet, Bill Gates, the Walton family (founders of Walmart), Ted Turner (founder of CNN), and David Rockefeller.

A small sampling of the numerous local and national philanthropic activities by the Mertz family over the years includes the following:

- In 1961, LuEsther Mertz founded *Choice Magazine Listening* for people with vision problems who are unable to read regular print. This non-profit organization selects articles, fiction, and poetry from contemporary periodicals, then records them and distributes them for free. To endow the organization, Mrs. Mertz set up a private foundation, called the Lucerna Fund.

- In 1969, Harold Mertz donated PCH's previous headquarters, located at the edge of historic Manhasset Bay, to the people of Port Washington through their Community Chest. This building, at 382 Main Street in Port Washington, was where the PCH staff resided from 1958 to 1967 and is now named the *Harold E. Mertz Community Center*.

- In 1980, Swarthmore College, near Philadelphia, received a $3 million donation for a new dormitory. This was where Harold Mertz went to college, and the dorm is appropriately named *Mertz Hall*.

- Swarthmore College also received renewable grants for two $250,000 scholarship funds for its students. These grants were set up in memory of the Mertz children. The scholarships are called the *Peter Mertz Scholarship* (initiated in 1955) and the *Joyce Mertz Gilmore Scholarship* (initiated in 1976).

- The *LuEsther T. Mertz Retinal Research Center,* located in the Manhattan Ear, Eye, & Throat Hospital, was opened and established in the 1980's. Its mission is to ensure the highest quality of care for sufferers of retinal disorders.

- In 1982, *The Joyce Theatre* in Manhattan, on Eighth Avenue at 19th Street, opened due to the support of LuEsther Mertz. The theatre, which is devoted to dance, was named in memory of her daughter Joyce who died of cancer in 1974.

- LuEsther Mertz was the chairwoman of Joseph Papp's New York Shakespeare Festival from 1973 to 1987, and she underwrote moving several of its productions from the Public Theater to Broadway. This included two very big-name and successful plays, *A Chorus Line* and *Two Gentlemen of Verona.*

- Throughout the 1980's, LuEsther Mertz contributed greatly to the revitalization of the New York Botanical Garden. At her death in 1991, sizeable gifts to the Botanical Garden from her estate as well as continued support through the LuEsther T. Mertz Charitable Trust made her one of the institution's largest benefactors. It has been written about Mrs. Mertz that "Without Publisher's Clearing House, the New York Botanical Garden might not have a library." If you have ever been there, you would know that the Botanical Garden's Library is no ordinary library. It is one of the largest and most important botanical and horticultural research libraries in the world, with over one million items including books, journals, original art and illustrations, seed and nursery catalogs, architectural plans of glass houses, scientific reprints, numerous photographs, and over 4,800 linear feet of archival materials. The Library serves as both a research facility and a public library, as well as a scholarly resource and source for general plant information. This world-class library is named *The LuEsther T. Mertz Library* in recognition of Mrs. Mertz's enduring financial commitment to the Botanical Garden, her dedicated support of the Garden's science programs, and her lifelong love of literature.

- In the 1980's, funds from Harold and Esther Mertz (Harold's second wife) helped purchase the Dunfermline Opera House, a 19th century theatre in Scotland, which was reconstructed inside the Aslo Center for the Performing Arts in Sarasota, Florida. This majestic 500-seat theatre is now named the *Mertz Theatre* and is associated with Florida State University.

- Harold Mertz loved Australian artwork, and he befriended and engaged the prominent art dealer Kym Bonython to purchase a comprehensive collection of works by Australian masters. This collection of 148 paintings was the largest and richest collection of modern Australian paintings located outside Australia. After the collection finished its tour of American galleries in 1973, Mr. Mertz donated them to the University of Texas in Austin. When Mr. Mertz was asked why he donated them to a college in Texas, he skirted the question by saying that he thought the lifestyles of Texas and Australia were similar, so they would be a good fit there. Due to a lack of space to show the paintings, in June 2000 the University of Texas and the Blanton Museum decided that the unique collection should be back in Australia where it could be seen and enjoyed by art lovers. The collection was auctioned off at Christie's, in Australia, for $15.9 million, a record amount for a personal collection of Australian artwork.

- In 2001, Esther Mertz donated $1 million to Rollins College via the establishment of the *Richard James Mertz Chair of Education*. This was in memory of her late son Richard (Harold's stepson), a 1960 graduate of Rollins College.

The Mertz family foundations are also major supporters of dozens of other organizations and charities including the Alzheimer's Disease and Related Disorders Association, St. Francis Hospital (in Roslyn, NY), Lincoln Center, the Central Park Conservatory, the American Civil Liberties Union, Stanford University, the Phoenix House Foundation, and many other worthwhile causes and institutions.

Part 1

Winning big prize money may seem like a dream come true. And for the most part, it is. Most families who win big money from Publishers Clearing House, or elsewhere for that matter, do well with their new-found wealth, but some do not fare so well.

One such impulsive soul was a young oil rig worker from Texas back in the 1970's who went completely hog wild after his big PCH win. This young man became worse off than before his windfall, ending up in debt and in jail. He had won our top prize at the time, $100,000, and immediately bought himself a fancy new car and a very fast speed boat. He soon received a number of speeding tickets, crashed both his new toys, and spent everything he had won and more – including binging on drugs and hookers. Rumor is that he didn't go to court for his speeding tickets, but instead took a shotgun and shot up the judge's home… which landed him in jail. Not too bright, I would say.

Then there was the sad case of the husband of one of our multi-million dollar winners. He reportedly spiraled downward into a drug habit, which eventually caused their divorce.

The final example of a big winner's misfortune is the most dastardly and reprehensible, although I am glad to say that it's not about a PCH winner. You may recall hearing about this story on national news. The story is about a forty-three-year-old truck driver who won $31 million in the Florida state lottery and went missing for many months. It was reported by CNN in January 2010 that this new multi-millionaire,

Abraham Shakespeare, was found buried under a concrete slab behind a friend's home in Plant City, Florida.

Fortunately, these kinds of sad stories for prize winners are not common. For the most part, PCH contest winners (and lottery winners) just have to put up with lots of new friends, relatives looking for loans, and marriage proposals from strangers.

Winner Celebrations at PCH Headquarters

Every year PCH's top prize winners are invited to spend a fun-filled weekend in New York, and we encourage them to bring their families to join in on the festivities. We call this our "Winners Weekend." Everything is paid for by PCH, and we treat the winners and their families like royalty. The long weekend usually includes a stay at the most elegant hotel in the city, The Plaza Hotel, overlooking Manhattan's Central Park, a first run Broadway show, and dinners at the finest restaurants. Dinner used to be at Windows On The World on the top floor of the World Trade Center before it disintegrated on September 11, 2001. The celebration also includes a grand party held in the cafeteria at PCH headquarters where all employees are invited to meet the winners. There are short speeches by the top brass, the presentation of the "Big Check" to the winners, and a tour of the building and the PCH operation.

Our lavish Winners Weekend tradition started in the late 1960's when our top prize winner, after receiving his check from PCH, called with the desire to come visit the company that had made him rich. Our winner wanted to fly in from Kentucky where he lived and personally thank the people who were responsible for his good fortune. The President of PCH at the time, Lou Kislik, discussed this potential visit with the rest of the management team. However, nobody was comfortable with the prospect of showing the winner around because they knew very little about him and had no idea what to expect. Each Vice President turned to one another and said, "You do it." Although no one wanted to entertain our contest winner, no one was sure how to tell him that he couldn't come for a visit. So reluctantly, Lou Kislik and Henry Cowen volunteered for the assignment.

Our winner from Kentucky paid for himself to get to New York and for his own lodging and entertainment. Lou took our contest winner on a tour of PCH headquarters and asked a couple of PCH employees to join them. Surprisingly, the tour turned out to be a tremendous success. The PCH staff enjoyed greeting the winner, and he got rounds and rounds of cheering and clapping as he went from department to department. At the same time, Lou and Henry unexpectedly enjoyed the visitor's company and his heartfelt expression of thanks. One of the employees on the tour suggested to Lou that we give future winners similar tours. Lou agreed, and from that point on all future winners were flown to New York for Winners Weekend, with one small change – all expenses were paid by PCH.

The all-employee party in the PCH cafeteria for Winners Weekend was always a lot of fun. In typical PCH style, we made this an event not to be missed. In the early years, champagne flowed freely in crystal glasses, and we served only the best hors d'oeuvres, like caviar and shrimp. There would be a speech by the PCH President and some funny winner stories told by Dave Sayer, head of the Prize Patrol. At times the winners said something, but more often than not they just stood there in absolute amazement as to their good fortune. At many of these parties we also held small cash prize drawings for PCH employees. We wanted PCH employees to see how it felt to win something.

Winners in the Big Apple

The weekend in Manhattan for the winners was always an adventure. Most winners had never been to Manhattan before, and many were from very small rural towns, so you can imagine what they thought of all the attention and Big Apple madness and frenzy. We always invited a PCH employee and his or her spouse to show the winner around the city, including dinner and a Broadway show. Of course, the PCH staff member and spouse were expected to stay at The Plaza for the weekend as well at PCH's expense.

Bernice Loew, one of our executive secretaries and a twenty-five year PCH veteran, often chaperoned the winners during their stay in New York

City. Bernice made it a point to arrive at the hotel earlier than our guests/ winners to deal with any unforeseeable happenings, of which there were many. She shared a couple of particularly amusing stories.

On one particular occasion, Bernice was waiting at The Plaza for our winner from Nebraska who was checking in soon. Bernice had an inkling from having spoken with our winner during the weeks prior to his arrival that he might be an "interesting" fellow, and sure enough, her intuition was dead on. Amid the beautiful people in the hotel lobby, a lone mid-westerner showed up... dressed in full farmer's gear.

There he stood, in an old, soiled pair of overalls and a checkered shirt, looking like he had just plowed the back forty. His teeth were missing, and he carried a small, tattered tote. When Bernice inquired as to other luggage, he replied in his heavy mid-western twang, "Nope – just what's in this 'ere bag. Didn't even bring mah teeth cuz' I'm fixin' ta order me a big steak, and I hear it's soft as butter so's I might as well leave the teeth in the drawer." Bernice knew right then and there that dinner that night at Windows On The World was going to be a big problem. Typical attire for men at this elegant, one-of-a-kind restaurant was a suit; even gentlemen wearing a sport jacket and tie were frowned upon.

Thinking on her feet, Bernice insisted that her new friend go shopping with her. Of course, she took him to one of the best clothing stores in the city. It took a bit of convincing, but they bought suitable clothing for the dinner party (on PCH), but not without a lot of backtalk and fretting about, "What am I gonna do wit' these new clothes once I git back home?"

Another winner's story Bernice likes to tell began when Bernice got a phone call from the very unhappy concierge at The Plaza. The concierge said to Bernice, his voice dripping in disdain, "There is someone here at the desk using your name and trying to check into the hotel." Apparently, our contest winner had no paperwork with her, no identification, no hotel confirmation, and no credit cards or money either. She just kept repeating to the concierge, "This he-yer Buhneese laydee say-ed I shud jis come he-yer 'n' go tuh mah room, 'n' that's whast I'm a-fixin' tuh do."

Part of the confusion was that this particular prize winner was from the deep south and was clearly out of her element. Her southern drawl was so strong that she may as well have been speaking another language. At this point our guest was getting rather boisterous and creating a scene at this fashionable New York City landmark. After a great deal of explanation over the phone and some rather ruffled feathers, Bernice convinced the concierge that she would be there shortly to help our guest, and that in fact, this individual was pre-registered to occupy a room there.

When Bernice arrived, she resolved the issues and helped the winner check in. Our winner got ready for dinner but not before taking everything out of the mini-bar in her room and putting all the small bottles of liquor and tiny bags of chips into her valise. All ended well when everyone assembled in Bernice's suite for a pre-dinner cocktail party, where everyone indulged in very expensive French wine before going out to dinner.

What Do a Man with a Monkey and a Man in Army Fatigues Have in Common?

The answer... both showed up at PCH headquarters one day saying they had won the big prize in the Publishers Clearing House contest.

The first incident was hysterically funny and was shared by the good-natured, congenial Bill Johnson, who loved a good prank, but this surpassed even his imagination. Bill put in over twenty years at PCH as head of Human Resources. The second event, told by respected Tom Lagan, a former Vice President, and friendly Bob McGoff, was downright terrifying.

IN THE LATE 1970's, a young man roller skated up Channel Drive, the main thoroughfare leading to PCH headquarters, with a live monkey on his back, and proceeded to enter the front lobby. Bill Johnson saw this very strange and comical vision out his office window, which had a clear view of the front entrance and street leading to PCH. So when Bill was called to handle the situation, he knew this was no ordinary guest.

Bill welcomed the visitor in wonderment, barely able to stop himself from laughing. Bill was sure there was more to the situation than met the eye, and he eagerly awaited the bizarre caller's explanation. The visitor showed Bill the PCH mailing piece, insistent that not only did it have his famous monkey's name on it, but that it was the winning entry as well!

Bill surmised that his newfound friend had probably ordered something in his monkey's name from another direct marketing company and it somehow found its way onto our mailing list. Bill kindly told the man and his monkey, still trying not to laugh, that it was not the winning entry. This comical visitor and his monkey companion took the news well, and then departed as they had arrived – the young man roller skated around the pond and down the street with the monkey on his back. It was an experience that to this day Bill will never forget.

In the early 1990's, a young man made the long walk up Channel Drive dressed in full army camouflage, right down to his army boots, carrying an ominous looking large duffel bag over his shoulder. He approached the lobby of PCH headquarters looking for his $10 million. Tom Lagan, who could be an imposing figure at 6 foot 4 inches tall, 220 pounds, and all solid muscle, was called to handle the situation. Upon seeing this menacing looking stranger, Tom immediately decided to call for backup. Tom called co-worker Bob McGoff, a strapping, fearless, young Irishman, to assist him with the situation. And just to play it safe, a Port Washington police detective was also asked to help.

For Bob McGoff, the mere fact that Tom Lagan elicited his help was disconcerting in and of itself. Both Tom and Bob had exactly the same thought: "I wonder what in the world this guy has in his duffel bag?" All three men, Tom, Bob, and the police detective, wondered when this guy was going to break out an Uzi from that damn bag.

To say this incident was tense would be an understatement. Tom Lagan and the detective explained to this man that he hadn't won the $10 million. The stranger in army fatigues never raised his voice. In fact, his demeanor was very calm, and his speech was completely monotone in nature, which made them all even more uneasy about what might happen next.

Tom Lagan kindly offered to pay his transportation home or to wherever he wanted to go. No one recalls if he accepted this offer, but our scary looking visitor then simply got up and left of his own accord.

They all anxiously watched him walk around the front circle and pond, and then down the long street leading away from PCH. It was like he was walking away in slow motion, and they watched his each and every step as he marched down the street. All three had the exact same thought – they were sure he was going to turn around and open fire on the three of them. To their astonishment and immense relief, he didn't.

The Birth of the Prize Patrol

Television advertising was first tested at PCH in the mid-1970's and was an immediate success. The goal of the television commercials was to bolster the consumer's belief that real people win by showing the real winners in the ads. These first commercials simply showed a portrait-like picture of our winners and indicated that you could also win cars, boats, and cash in the Publishers Clearing House sweepstakes. We supported the two largest mailings of the year, right after the January 1st and the July 4th holidays, with massive amounts of television advertising, and this produced more orders, more non-order entries, and more profit. In addition, an unintended side effect was a much higher profile for PCH with the public and the media.

Then in 1988 the PCH Advertising department, consisting of Dave Sayer, the manager of the two-person department, and his young assistant, Todd Sloane, were looking into new ways to create more interesting television commercials featuring the PCH winners. Although our contest winners were generally nice people, when it came time to filming them in our television commercials, they always appeared stiff and staged in front of the camera. This wasn't really surprising since they weren't actors.

We had just had the latest drawing for our newest big contest winner. Dave and Todd were talking about the newest millionaire, who was from Texas, and Todd simply said to his boss, Dave, "I have an idea."

PCH had taught all of us to have an open mind to new ideas, and Dave was no exception, so he innocently replied, "What is it?"

Todd then responded, "You're about to place a phone call to a guy in Texas to tell him he won a million dollars. Then maybe you'll bring him to New York and film a TV commercial where he'll sit woodenly in front of a camera and say something like, 'I just won a million dollars in the Publishers Clearing House Sweepstakes – You can, too.' I think we could make more exciting TV advertising if we surprised him with the Big Check at his front door."

At first, Dave thought the idea seemed totally implausible, but Todd volunteered to help and also suggested he could use his new amateur camcorder. So instead of calling the next winner on the phone and bringing him to New York as usual to film a TV commercial, Dave and Todd flew to Texas to surprise and record the reaction of our newest millionaire, John Yancy and his wife, Julie. Dave drove the van, and Todd held the shaky, hand-held camera.

If they had had a shy or reserved winner that day, it would have been the first and last Prize Patrol trip. But it turned out that the winner's enthusiasm and excitement were contagious when caught on film. The winner's wife, Julie, shrieked with excitement, and the winner's entire family jumped up and down in disbelief. Emmy Award winning actors could not have given the Prize Patrol better footage for their TV commercials, wobbly recording and all.

When Dave and Todd got back home, they knew they had captured something special. Before the final decision was made, however, we had some focus groups observe the winning moment captured on film. Every single person in the focus groups loved the new commercials – and the legendary Prize Patrol was born. Although the goal was to generate more excitement, orders, and profit from our TV commercials, which it did, it also added to the renown of Publishers Clearing House.

In the very early days, Dave and Todd wore plain blue blazers without a PCH emblem, the black van didn't have the large PCH logo on it, nor were balloons, red roses, or champagne used. These were soon added to help with the winning moment. Initially, the Prize Patrol filmed live footage for the commercials and would take their time editing the video before turning it into a commercial for national TV. Later on, however, after the Prize Patrol got good at surprising people, we took it one step further. On some of their excursions, we started implementing truly live commercials where the ads were aired at the precise moment of the surprise as well (with no time for editing, etc). With this came the challenging technical aspect of a truly live TV commercial with the added equipment such as a large uplink satellite truck and production vehicle.

Over time, the renown of the Prize Patrol grew and so did the number of Prize Patrol trips. Up to about twenty times each year, the Prize Patrol travels the country to surprise PCH winners. The winners are never notified in advance, so the surprise is completely genuine. No matter where you are, the Prize Patrol will find you… that's absolutely guaranteed!

Dave Sayer has presented virtually every major prize for almost thirty years and describes his job at PCH as such, "No matter how many winners we surprise or how much money we give away, it's a thrill for us every single time." He has also commented, "I feel like we are on an adventure every time we go out to deliver a prize. While it is sometimes a challenge to track down people, someone is always willing to be an accomplice to help us make the surprise happen." The Prize Patrol adventures have made such exciting TV footage that even Oprah has shown interest in their escapades. Dave has been a guest on the Oprah show three times and has appeared on many other talk shows throughout his distinguished career as well.

As head of the illustrious Prize Patrol, Dave has probably logged more miles than perhaps any other man in history, and is as good-hearted a man as you'll ever meet. Dave Sayer himself wrote the lyrics and the melody for the catchy and emotional song heard in some of our TV commercials, called, "The House Where Dreams Come True." This tune was first used in the early 1990's, and consumers loved the song and its message. The lyrics are as follows:

Think about your daydreams and what you would do,
If you won a fortune, out of the blue.
Miracles can happen, can happen to you;
Publishers Clearing House, the house where dreams come true.

As to the fate of Todd Sloane, Dave's young assistant, he came to be known as our resident "creative genius" at PCH, with many more great ideas down the road. Interestingly, I was a Manager when Todd was a young entry level Marketing Analyst, and I remember Todd coming to see me for advice about shifting out of the Marketing department to the Advertising department. We had a very passionate one-on-one debate about his future at PCH, and I tried to convince him that he would be better off if he stayed put in the much larger Marketing department, but Todd thought otherwise. I hate to admit that I tried to talk him out of the move, and in hindsight, boy was I wrong! Todd did extraordinary things for PCH and currently has the well-deserved title of Senior Vice President (and to this day he still enjoys traveling on many of the Prize Patrol adventures).

Our Favorite Winner – Bob Castleberry ($10 million)

Bob Castleberry turned out to be the greatest goodwill ambassador that PCH could possibly have. When the Prize Patrol first surprised him in March 1989, we knew nothing about him except that he lived in Denton, Texas, which is about 35 miles north of Dallas. Before long, all of us at PCH, as well as the citizens of Denton, the whole state of Texas, and many throughout the entire country knew him, loved him, and admired him.

Bob's live winning moment was scheduled for the early evening, just minutes before the PCH commercial footage was to be aired during NBC's *Nightly News with Tom Brokaw*. There was a large group traveling with the Prize Patrol, including ad agency, public relations, and local media personnel, who crowded into the narrow stairwell leading to Bob's second floor apartment. Although they tried to be quiet, the noise from the horde of people and their cars and trucks must have gotten Bob's attention because he opened the door on the very first knock. As Bob saw the mob of people, the cameras, and the balloons, he said in a thick Texas drawl and with an impish grin, "Well, what have we got here?"

Dave then announced to him, "You've just won $10 million in the Publishers Clearing House Sweepstakes!"

Bob quickly responded, "Well, goll-eeee!" and then continued, "Well, come in! Please come in!" His big warm Texas accent, aided by his western attire of faded jeans and cowboy boots, were perfect for the cameras.

Bob was a natural in the spotlight and became an instant celebrity with national TV appearances from New York to Hollywood. He appeared on the *Letterman Show, Live with Regis and Kathie Lee, The Maury Povich Show*, and other top talk shows as well. Bob's jolly, happy-go-lucky style and large physical demeanor called to mind comedian Jonathan Winters.

Soon after his big win, Bob, a sixty-year old bachelor, started getting numerous friendly letters from females he never met, many with marriage proposals. He loved to chat about his new female friends with the talk show hosts, all the while maintaining he was a confirmed bachelor. Bob retired from his job as an account executive at Moore Business Forms and pursued the dream of his lifetime – to serve his beloved hometown of Denton. He ran for Mayor and won, and he was so popular that he served three consecutive terms, nurturing economic growth in his hometown.

Besides endowing scholarships in memory of his parents and donating generously to local charities, Bob also enjoyed his newfound wealth in style… purchasing a white $120,000 Rolls Royce, with red and white leather interior, and a beautiful 650-acre ranch. When Bob bought some cattle for his ranch, he fashioned the branding iron after the Publishers Clearing House logo. Now that was a nice touch!

Sadly, Bob passed away in October 2004. Dave Sayer summed it up best when he said about Bob, "Although I have known hundreds of our contest giveaway winners over the years, Bob stands out as one of the biggest – not only because of his robust build, but also because he had a heart and personality as big as Texas."

The First Live Super Bowl Winner – Mary Ann Brandt ($10 million)

This was another great idea pushed by Todd Sloane. The concept was to surprise our contest winner via a live commercial on Super Bowl Sunday. Senior management initially thought this suggestion was ridiculous and way too expensive. A winning moment filmed and aired completely live on Super Bowl Sunday would be a really big risk. The audience would be huge, and so much could go wrong! The winner might not be home, or could come to the door naked and wrapped in only a towel (now that wouldn't be so bad).

Todd can be very convincing, though, so we decided to give it a shot. The first live Super Bowl surprise was in late January 1995 and, as expected, was not easy to pull off. The closer it got to this first live event, D-Day as we called it, the more anxious Todd grew... because it was his idea to try this new tactic. The pressure was immense not to waste the large cost of the live 30-second shot to air on the Super Bowl's post-game show. We had looked at airing the commercial during the Super Bowl game itself, but the multi-million dollar cost to do this was just too risky.

It was up to Dave and Todd to accomplish this dicey undertaking. The first thing they needed to know was where the winner was from, and this presented the first obstacle. Contest rules were such that we couldn't determine the winner until a few days before the live commercial was aired. Dave and Todd anxiously awaited the winner selection and location so they could put their plan into action. When PCH finally made the $10 million winner selection, our newest millionaire was found to live in Phoenix, Arizona.

Now came the hard part. Would the winner be home on Super Bowl Sunday? Todd Sloane, in panic mode, made first contact with the unsuspecting winner. Todd said, "I called her house and hung up. I had to hear her voice."

The Prize Patrol team then discussed ways to find out in advance where the winner would be on D-Day. I should mention that Todd was not only a creative genius, but he also could be very sneaky. They decided to reach the winner, surreptitiously, through Carroll Rotchford, another member of the Prize Patrol team. Carroll called the winner, pretending to be a researcher doing a survey on Super Bowl commercials, and she made sure not to mention Publishers Clearing House. She told the soon-to-be millionaire that she would be paid $50 if the researchers could call her during the game and ask her opinion of the commercials. The winner said that would be fine, but then mentioned that she'd be at her son's house watching the game. Now panic set in again! They knew where the winner lived… but where did the son live? Thinking quickly, Carroll asked for the son's phone number, and made up a story that his address was needed as well in order to send the $50 check to that location.

A day or so later, the Prize Patrol team flew from New York to Arizona, rented a vehicle at the local airport, and on Super Bowl Sunday nervously headed out in their black van. The large plastic decal for the Prize Patrol van would be attached later. They had already learned not to attach the PCH logo too early. On the way to surprise a winner once, the Prize Patrol team got hungry, so they stopped at a McDonald's drive-thru window. The cashier got really flustered and excited because she thought the Prize Patrol was there for her.

For this first ever PCH Super Bowl surprise, the Prize Patrol was accompanied by an army of trucks and people. This included a large satellite truck, an enormous production vehicle, crews from *Dateline NBC* and *Extra*, reporters from *People Magazine*, plus the local press. The entourage was told to park a few blocks away so as not to tip off the surprise. All of the activity, however, caught the attention of many curious onlookers. Todd, thinking on his feet, appeased the observers by saying they were taping a commercial. One gawker said, "Oh darn, I thought you were the Prize Patrol."

When the moment arrived, this very large group converged at the winner's son's front door. Our winner, Mary Ann Brandt, opened the door and was surprised and totally speechless. We found out later that Mary Ann didn't say much because she had a mouthful of chicken when she answered the door. The winner's reaction didn't make great TV, but the Prize Patrol team was relieved that nothing bad happened. The fact that this feat could all be arranged and pulled off in so little time was no less than a miracle. Back at PCH, we were happy with the free extra publicity this event produced.

The Beautiful Girl in the Towel

You may be wondering about the picture on the front cover and whether this incident is real or fake. The truth is, the story as well as the winning moment and the national commercials that were aired are absolutely, positively, 100% real. However, PCH would not grant me the rights to reproduce the photo of our alluring enchantress, so the picture on the cover is a simulation of the real event. Here is lovely Courtney's captivating story.

Million dollar winner Martha McMillen, from a small Missouri town, wasn't home when the Prize Patrol, with video camera in hand, started knocking at her door in July 1996. However, hearing a persistent knock at the door, Martha's eighteen-year old daughter Courtney jumped from her bath, wrapped herself in a towel, and still dripping wet, opened the front door. It was what you would call the surprise of a lifetime, and it was all caught on tape for national television.

Courtney's shocked reaction couldn't have been rehearsed... and it certainly didn't hurt that Courtney was a drop-dead gorgeous young lady with an infectious heart-warming smile. I am not sure who was more surprised, Courtney, who thought it was her seven-year old brother who was prone to locking himself out, or Dave Sayer of the Prize Patrol, when this beautiful young lady opened the door wrapped only in a towel. After Courtney got over the shock of the situation, she innocently explained, "In our town, it's no big deal cause we know everybody."

Consumers across the country loved the live television commercial, as did the news media. Courtney's story and towel-clad image were in the news everywhere including a feature story in the Magazine section of *The New York Times*. And excitement about Courtney's natural beauty even came from a very unlikely source – the Elite Modeling Agency. This first-class modeling agency thought Courtney looked like an "American Nicole Kidman" and wanted to meet her. So when Courtney and her family came to New York for winners weekend, we set up an appointment in Manhattan with the prestigious agency. It turned out Courtney was gorgeous enough, and we knew that, but sadly, she was too short at 5 feet 2 inches tall, so the modeling agency didn't sign her.

Father Mike Berner ($1 million)

The small rural town of Earling, Iowa, with a total population of only 466 people, was about to meet the Prize Patrol. In fact, the Prize Patrol team for this trip included a group of about thirty people. Included were TV personality and *ABC News* reporter Joan Lunden with her production team who wanted to be in on the surprise. The Prize Patrol left New York on August 19th and were about to learn what a hot, steaming, Iowa summer day would feel like. It was a sweltering 100 degrees when Father Mike was surprised.

On August 20, 1998, Father Mike Berner became the most famous and wealthiest small town priest in the United States when he won $1 million in the PCH sweepstakes. A lot of faith and some luck paid off for Father Mike, who was the pastor of St. Joseph's Church in this tiny farming town. Within fifteen minutes after Father Mike was told the good news, just about the entire town gathered on the front lawn of the church to celebrate with the lucky man. The surprise was telecast live on NBC's *Nightly News with Tom Brokaw*. In addition, Father Mike was featured on Joan Lunden's *Behind Closed Doors* program.

Bright and early the very next morning after his big win, the thirty-eight year old priest told parishioners at his 8:00 a.m. Mass that it was time for things to get back to normal. Father Mike later informed the press that he planned to put part of his winnings toward the installation of an air conditioning system in St. Joseph's Church, humbly explaining in his mid-western accent what the Prize Patrol had just found out – that the heat of the Iowa summers can be "one little ordeal."

Father Mike also said of his windfall, "We're going to stick to our day job," however he soon embarked on some fascinating contest winner adventures. In typical PCH fashion, we flew Father Mike to New York for an all-expense paid weekend celebration. Joining him was his friend, Father Tom Crowley. During the Winner Weekend festivities, Father Mike appeared on the *The Rosie O'Donnell Show* (October 1998), where he and Father Tom sang an off-key version of "Sweet Caroline" with none other than Neil Diamond himself, Rosie's other guest that day.

In addition to fancy dinners at the famous Lutece and the Four Seasons restaurants, a Broadway show, and a party at PCH headquarters, the two priests also enjoyed the Yankees' victory parade in lower Manhattan. The Yankees had won the World Series that year. However, the highlight of the trip for Father Mike and Father Tom was their breakfast with Cardinal O'Connor at his residence and then attending Sunday Mass at St. Patrick's Cathedral.

A few weeks later, Father Mike flew back to New York to appear on the *David Letterman Show* (November 1998), matching wits with the late night host.

From what I am told, clergy wins at PCH are not unusual. Several clergymen have won prizes in the PCH sweepstakes over the years, but I don't think any have been as charming as Father Mike. Everyone who met Father Mike, including the celebrities he met, were struck by his wonderful sense of humor.

4   My Early Days

I started working at PCH in 1973 at the young age of twenty-one. At the time, PCH was still a very small company. There were only about 40 professional level employees, plus we had a clerical/operational staff of around 100 employees who handled customer calls and letters, processed the incoming mail (both orders and non-orders), ran our data processing equipment, and a lettershop for our first-class billing program. All operational functions were handled entirely in-house as we were able to handle all work internally without any outsourcing.

My initial job was as an entry level Marketing Analyst; there were only three of us in those early days and our job was to fully analyze all promotional mailings and every test. Our reports contained detailed results and conclusions on what worked and what didn't work, and each and every mailing and test got its own separate comprehensive write-up, which went to the entire senior management team.

Soon after I started, the workload became incredibly challenging due to the company's significant growth. In a relatively short span of time, we went from one mailing a month to twelve mailings a month, an astounding twelve-fold increase in the workload. This dramatic increase occurred so quickly that staff additions never even came close to matching the upsurge in activity, but we continued to report on everything in full detail. For the most part, I worked very long hours. A typical week for me included ten-hour days Monday through Friday, plus I brought lots of work home over the weekend. That's what most of us did, and we loved doing it.

In spite of the impossible workload, PCH was a great place to work, as you'll see from the stories and anecdotes told in this chapter and throughout the book.

My Very First Day on the Job... I Ask for a Raise

I started looking for a full-time job right after I graduated from college. To be suitable for my interviews in the business world, I had no choice but to say good-bye to my long, pony-tailed hair and traumatically had my first haircut in four years. I also had to buy my first business suit.

My interview at PCH was with Alan Rabinowitz, Vice President of Finance, who was also in charge of the very small Marketing Analysis department. I had never worked in an office or business setting before, as my summer jobs were either as a camp counselor or mowing grass for the Town Parks department. Mr. Rabinowitz hired me, and to this day I am not sure why. My first day at PCH was July 23, 1973. At the time, I knew absolutely nothing about Publishers Clearing House... and had no idea I was embarking on a remarkable thirty-year long roller coaster ride.

On my very first day on the job, I did something incredibly naïve – I decided to ask for a raise. My twin brother, Dennis, had started working a few weeks before me at an insurance company in Manhattan, and his starting salary was more than mine. I thought that just wasn't fair! I wish I could say that I was being bold, but that would be a lie. In hindsight, I can say without hesitation that asking for a raise on my first day on the job was the dumbest thing I ever did. But that's what I did.

My starting salary was $7,300 a year, or $140 a week. That was back in 1973 and while this compensation was not bad for the times, my twin brother had a starting salary of $7,800. My highly competitive nature was at stake here, so in the afternoon on the day I started, I went to see my boss, Alan Rabinowitz. I said hello, mentioned that I was enjoying my first day, and then politely continued, "Thanks for hiring me, Mr. Rabinowitz, but I think I should be paid more."

After a very long pause and stunned in total disbelief, Mr. Rabinowitz finally replied, "Let me think about it and get back to you." I must say that this was the only time throughout the rest of my long career at PCH that I ever remember seeing Alan speechless.

The next day Alan called me into his office to say he had decided to increase my salary to $7,500 per year. I was thrilled and enthusiastically thanked him. If you do the math, that's a raise of 14 cents an hour (or less than $6 per week). It's amazing that so little could make one happy in those days. I will admit that to this day, I am grateful that my boss didn't kick me out altogether on that very first day. It turned out that Alan was a great teacher, and he became a wonderful friend and mentor to me.

The Hiring Process

Portraying the unique atmosphere at Publishers Clearing House to those who never worked there is extraordinarily challenging, and it started with the unusual hiring process.

If a person passed the typical PCH interviews, then he or she had to go through an entire day of psychological testing with an industrial psychologist named Sid Koran. I learned in time that PCH only hired employees who scored within the top 2% of the population on the intelligence scale. Everyone at PCH was unusually bright, so this may have been true. However, since they hired me, I know this wasn't entirely accurate. I was a straight "B" student at college, although I did get all "A's" in my major (Mathematics). I know I wasn't in the top 2%, so when I was hired it must have been because Alan Rabinowitz saw something in that inexperienced, young kid.

I have spoken with many former PCH employees, and they have all said similar things about the enthralling PCH environment. A comment from Jack Brittain typifies the feelings held by all former PCH employees. This one-time PCH manager subsequently held a senior management role at Time Inc. and became a respected publishing industry executive. He said the following about his short time at PCH:

"I met and became friends with some of the most brilliant people I have ever encountered." He also went on to say, "PCH was one of those workplaces that most everyone in direct marketing held up as a 'paradise' place to work. The fact that you were good enough to pass PCH's rigorous 'entrance exam' of testing, psychological interviewing, and more testing, was an attest to your high intellect and abilities. If you were offered a job within the PCH paradise, and nearly all who were offered a position accepted it, the perception was that you were 'golden.'"

The Management Team

If I had to describe the management team in three words, they would be playful, eccentric, and demanding. The senior executives were as unique and interesting a group as you will ever meet.

One small example was the strong urging that all managers or potential managers go through Est, a very popular and widespread movement in the 1970's founded by Werner Erhard. Est stands for Erhard Seminar Training and is also Latin for "it is." The principal goal was to give participants, in a very brief time, a sense of personal transformation and enhanced power. It also included taking responsibility for one's life with an emphasis on integrity. Est's approach was often abusive, profane, demeaning, and authoritarian. The training was known, for example, for locking participants in a large seminar room, not allowing them use of a bathroom, and yelling at the trainees. I don't know how effective this movement or training was, but going through the Est training was encouraged by our President at the time, Lou Kislik, and one of our Vice Presidents, John Mienik. The end result was that the atmosphere from the Est training permeated the top and middle management levels at PCH. I was lucky to be too new and too junior at the time to be "invited" to go through this challenging but supposedly life changing training.

In some measure due to the Est training, but primarily due to the philosophy of Harold Mertz, the company invited open thought and discussion no matter what level you were or what job you had. In fact, the senior management team was known to debate, rather heatedly, not only important issues, but even the not-so-important matters. It was also common for the Vice Presidents to take turns arguing different sides of an issue. This debating style was a favorite of my first boss, Alan Rabinowitz. No matter what position you had, he would always take the other side. I think they invented the phrase, "devil's advocate" for Alan. The end result was that we always fully discussed an issue, and this worked well for our growing business.

The senior management group was also incredibly demanding of all employees. This was partly because the business was growing amazingly fast and there was always too much to do. But it wasn't just the exponentially increasing workload. The Vice Presidents, for their part, each had a very demanding personal style. In fairness, hard work, although expected, was also rewarded.

Lastly, it was the delightful mischievousness of the management team that contributed in large part to the wonderful environment and camaraderie at PCH, and made it such a great place to work.

The Camaraderie and the PCH Culture

You could not find a closer group of employees than those at Publishers Clearing House. Virtually all former PCH colleagues have told me that they felt as if they were treated like a member of a large family and also that they felt like a part owner of the company. The following three examples should give you a sense of the camaraderie and underlying spirit at PCH.

In 1982, the company sponsored a farewell party for Sue Cook, one of our Human Resource Managers. Sue was single, attractive, and always enjoyed the PCH fun, but was leaving for a new job in Vermont, so a party was in order. In an effort to portray the kind of men our luscious, single colleague would meet in Vermont, our esteemed Treasurer, Dan Doyle, made a memorable appearance and speech at Sue's farewell celebration. Dan gave his playful speech in full costume, dressed as a fictitious character he called Amos Woodcock. He sported a coonskin cap, lumber jacket, black boots, bikini underwear (no pants), and he carried a large chain saw. Around his neck he wore a necklace that he had fashioned as a gift for Sue... a wood-carved penis. It was all in fun, and it was hysterically funny. You definitely couldn't do that today! The following are two pictures from that event that I hope capture at least a part of the fun we had.

PCH Treasurer, Dan Doyle
AKA Amos Woodcock

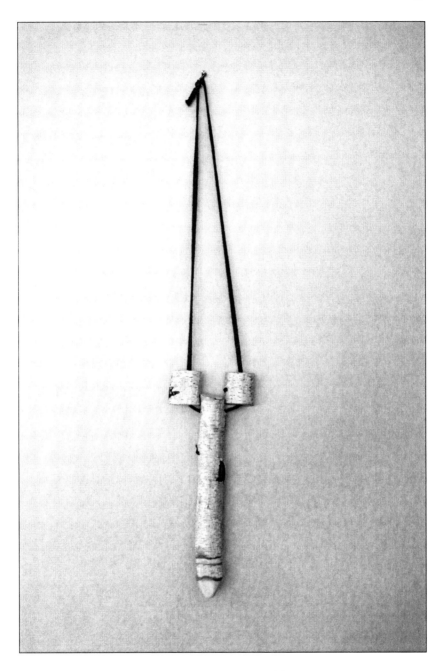

Amos Woodcock necklace
Gift presented to Sue Cook

Another example of how close we felt concerns my well-regarded colleague Norman Nahigian. In 1999, we had our first ever layoffs after many years of unabated growth in sales and staff size. Norman had been working at PCH for thirty years in the Information Services department, was a Senior Director, and had a staff of 30 to 40 employees in programming reporting to him. Norman's knowledge was too valuable, so he was not on the list of employees targeted for the first round of layoffs/early retirement. Upon seeing which staff members were being let go, Norman went to see his boss, Steve Miller, Vice President of Information Services. Norman told Steve, "I would like to take early retirement so that a few members of my staff can be saved." This was a truly astonishing request, but it typifies how we all felt about our colleagues. Steve tried to talk him out of taking "early retirement," but Norman was adamant. To this day, Norman is fondly referred to by PCH employees as "the living legend," not just for his act of benevolence that day, but also because of his unending willingness at PCH to accomplish whatever was put before him, especially by the ever-demanding Marketing department.

A third and final example of our family-like culture was the retirement party in 1987 for beloved PCH Vice President, Alan Rabinowitz. For over twenty years, Alan was Vice President of Finance, but due to health reasons he was retiring early at age fifty-four. Everyone knew this party was going to be a special, eventful evening, due to the playful, argumentative, and colorful nature of the guest of honor. Virtually everyone who worked at PCH showed up, including secretaries, clerical workers, managers, directors, and vice presidents. Even many former PCH colleagues called and begged to get an invite to what was likely to be the party of the century.

As the celebration took place, ten long, hilarious speeches roasting Alan were given, primarily by many of our unique senior management team. In describing Alan's cantankerous style, one executive joked, "Alan stayed awake during his recent bypass surgery to tell the doctor he could have done it better."

Another funny speech came from one of Alan's secretaries, Rita Powers, an attractive redhead. Rita talked about Alan's engaging personality, delivering her monologue as well as any great talk show host. Rita passionately revealed, "Alan lusted after food the way some men lusted after women." And then, with tears in her eyes and staring at Alan in the audience, she followed with, "But he never looked at me the way he looked at food." Then there was a long pause, and Rita's tears turned to a sinister grin, as she went on to explain, "But his wife Lucille confided in me. When she is in the mood, she just puts chocolate mousse on the nightstand, and that does the trick."

The most outrageous part of the celebration was when Alan Rabinowitz himself and another Vice President, Tom Owens, started to do a strip tease in front of the entire large, unruly, and by then mostly drunken crowd. Tom, an older, very dapper gentleman, initiated it, but Alan, who never liked to be topped, kept it going. Of course, the strip tease took place to appropriately played sleazy music and many catcalls and screams from the women in the crowd to, "Take it all off!" First the ties came off, then the shirts, then the shoes and socks, then Tom's gold chains, then the belts. Alan and Tom kept egging each other on to the loud cheers of the wild crowd. When the strip tease was finally over, it was not a pretty sight! I wish I had some pictures of that tantalizing event to share, but they would have been censored anyway.

At the end of the night, Alan finally got his chance to thank the rowdy crowd. He gave the best one-liner of the night, and there were many. Alan said to the group, in his typical sarcastic style, "I have gotten thirty-two gifts so far, and the total value is only $1.89."

Alan passed away way too early in his retirement. I miss him dearly, but am fortunate to still be in touch with his lovely wife, Lucille.

Lou Kislik

On a less risqué note, I don't know how many company Presidents take the time out of their hectic schedules to give new employees a personal tour of corporate headquarters and company operations. In the early years at PCH, every quarter or so, our President did just that. My tour in 1973 was with Lou Kislik, with whom I am still in touch today.

Lou was an extraordinary leader and President. Everyone loved and respected him, as he steadfastly led PCH to consistent growth. Lou's background in statistics and computers was perfectly suited to the company's needs in the '60's and '70's, as we were building a data-driven, research-oriented, world-class direct marketing enterprise. Lou was known for his approachability, openness, kindness, intelligence, and integrity.

Lou's connection to PCH actually started with the company's founders. Lou met Joyce Mertz, the daughter of Harold and LuEsther Mertz, when they were both young college students at Swarthmore College, and Lou became good friends with the Mertz family. After college, Lou went to Wharton Business School where he got an MBA with a major in Statistics, and subsequently went to work for IBM. Soon after Lou's career started at IBM, Mr. Mertz called Lou to ask him to come to work for PCH. But after a long discussion, they both agreed that it wasn't the right time. A few years later, Mr. Mertz called Lou again, and this time, the time was right. Lou was brought on board in 1962, and his scientific background served PCH extremely well, especially in those early growth years.

Several years later, in 1969, Lou became acting President of the company when Harold Mertz took a six month vacation to Australia. Before Harold Mertz left for this long trip, however, Joyce Mertz had an unusual request for her dad – that he sign a contract indicating that she and Lou were totally in charge, and that when her dad came back he would continue to let them run the company. Joyce was worried that her dad, known as a very hands-on person, would usurp their jobs upon his return. Mr. Mertz signed the agreement and lived up to his promise. Lou remained as President, and from that point on, Harold Mertz was never actively involved in the running of the company.

I have such fond memories of Lou's leadership and personality. My fondest personal memory in addition to my PCH tour was seeing Lou driving to work one day in his brand new car... a magnificent, shiny, silver blue Ferrari. The rumor was that the Ferrari was a bonus from Harold Mertz, but I don't know if that's true or not. Lou used to bring the car into the warehouse at PCH headquarters, and you would see him in a striking pinstripe suit, cigar in his mouth, peering under the hood of his car and tinkering with the sophisticated mid-engine.

Shockingly, Lou left PCH very abruptly in 1978. We came in one morning and were stunned by the news that spread like wildfire. Our beloved President, Lou Kislik, had left… no party, no goodbyes, no explanation, no nothing. We were just told that Lou wasn't President anymore. This was most unusual at PCH, and the feeling throughout the building was as if a close friend or family member had just died. This surprise came just two years after the Direct Marketing Association awarded Lou with their highest honor: Marketer of the Year (1976).

It was not until many years later that I learned that Lou had had a serious disagreement with LuEsther Mertz, who was General Partner at the time. From what I have been told, the owners were worried about a new competitor, American Family Publishers, and wanted to know how PCH was going to deal with this unwanted newcomer. The Executive Committee, primarily LuEsther Mertz and Bill Rennert, wanted PCH to fight the new competitor aggressively and do whatever it took to combat their entry into our marketplace. But Lou's philosophy was completely different. He believed that PCH should go about being the best at who we were, rather than doing anything too aggressive or of questionable nature. This philosophical difference was the cause of the dispute, and LuEsther fired Lou.

I should note that many years later, a PCH Executive Committee member approached Lou and apologized for allowing him to be fired. It is very clear that the aggressive tactics PCH was later to employ would not have occurred under Lou's watch, and if he hadn't left, it would have likely changed PCH's entire future… and perhaps even the future of the whole direct marketing community.

The Perks

Very few, if any, companies have ever treated its employees better than Publishers Clearing House. Some of the perks at PCH were typical, but some were quite unusual. The most remarkable perk, which I have never heard done at any other company, was fresh cut flowers on each employee's desk every Monday morning. This idea came directly from Harold Mertz himself.

The most generous perk was what we called the PSRP, which stands for "Profit Sharing/Retirement Plan." The company guaranteed to put an amount equal to 7% of our salary into our retirement account each year, but this was not the unusual part. The extraordinary aspect was that for many, many years in a row, PCH more than doubled that contribution and put in 15% instead. We would be informed annually about the extra contribution in a memo to all employees. This letter would state that results were so good that the Executive Committee had decided to put in additional dollars to our retirement accounts. This was quite generous, and the 15% contribution by PCH was, in fact, the maximum allowed under IRS regulations.

There were also the more traditional type perks like all-day access to free coffee and soda, an annual Christmas bonus for all employees (cold hard cash in your paycheck), free turkeys for Thanksgiving, a generous expense account for lunches around town with clients or your fellow co-workers, and tons of special corporate events. The special company-sponsored events and activities included skating parties on our pond in front of the building, an annual company picnic at a local park, a weekly bowling league, softball games, bake-offs (where everyone cooked their favorite dessert), tennis and volleyball leagues, aerobics classes, parties for the big prize winners with all PCH employees in our cafeteria, an employee written quarterly Newsletter, and much more. Of course, as with most companies back then, there were lots of Friday night drinking parties as well.

Publishers Clearing House also wanted to let its employees know what it felt like to be a winner. So in addition to the random cash prizes at the Winner Celebrations of which I already mentioned, we also held a monthly employee drawing for one of a dozen or so four foot plants that were on display each month in the common areas. This did present a problem though. These tall plants were always a challenge loading into your car, especially for those like me who drove a small compact car.

One of the favorite perks for most employees was "corn day," which was established as an annual event by our President, Lou Kislik, and Bill Johnson, head of Human Resources. Bill was born and raised on a Long Island farm, and his family still grew corn for a living. Once a year during harvest time, PCH bought a huge amount of corn from Bill's family farm. Bill made sure that the corn was just picked that morning, and PCH employees volunteered to shuck the corn while our Maintenance department did the cooking in huge vats in the parking lot of PCH headquarters. There was enough corn-on-the-cob for employees to eat all they wanted, and it was, without a doubt, the freshest and sweetest corn I have ever tasted.

The management team's favorite perk was being able to take our spouses on a free vacation as they accompanied us twice a year on the direct marketing conventions around the country. My favorite places were New Orleans, Las Vegas, and Los Angeles.

Another nice little perk was the free ride to and from the train station if you were commuting from Manhattan or Queens. Employees who took the train to work in the morning were picked up at the local train station for the five-minute ride to PCH headquarters. At the end of the day, you could also be driven back to the train station. In the very early days, the transportation was a grey station wagon with the license plate PCH-1, driven by George, from Maintenance. In those early days, we all wore lots of different hats.

Lastly, PCH generously paid to further our college education. For me, I attained my MBA at night from Adelphi University in 1980, courtesy of PCH.

My Brother Almost Gives our Receptionist a Nervous Breakdown

After I was working at PCH for a few years, a comical incident happened that is worth sharing. At the time, it was still a very small company, and due to the close-knit working environment, everyone knew each other quite well. This was especially true for Helen, our front lobby receptionist. She was a very kind and affable woman in her sixties, always smiling and cheerfully greeting visitors and employees.

My daily routine was to come in the front entrance of PCH headquarters, and Helen and I would chat for a few moments before I started my long day. I would see Helen many times each day, not only when I arrived in the morning but also when I passed through the lobby for a meeting on the other side of the building.

One day, my identical twin brother Dennis came to visit. He came in the front entrance, went up to Helen and said, "I'm here to see Darrell Lester."

From what I am told, Helen got very flustered, her face turned white as a ghost, and she asked him to repeat what he had just said.

My brother repeated, "Can I see Darrell Lester?"

Still extremely flustered, Helen called me on my extension. She sounded like she was having a nervous breakdown. She said to me, "There is someone here asking for Darrell Lester, but you're Darrell Lester, but Darrell Lester is standing right in front of me."

I quickly came out to greet my exact lookalike brother. Helen apparently didn't know I had an identical twin brother. She was very relieved when I introduced him to her as such.

My One and Only Mistake at PCH

I am very proud of my long-standing reputation at PCH. I was known for never making a mistake and was never late on a project or assignment. Because of this reputation, whenever there was a critically important project to get done or something was extremely time-sensitive, it would almost always be given to me. There were many times later in my career when I would be asked to manage certain projects, even those totally out of my area of responsibility, because of the critical nature or sensitivity of the project.

Now I am sure that no one remembers this but me, but I did make a mistake once, very early in my career at PCH. What I didn't know at the time was that this mistake worked in my favor.

I had been at PCH for about a year at the time and was doing a very detailed and lengthy project for Mike Kaufman, one of our long-time Vice Presidents. This was a two-month long project in which I reported on the results of all our outside lists for the past year. The report was an oversized spreadsheet that was about sixty pages long with hundreds of numbers and indices on each page. This was in 1974, well before desktop computers, and every calculation had to be done manually and then posted to the spreadsheet. I worked long and hard on it. The report would be used to determine what lists to use for the next year.

I handed in the effort, after two months, right on time, of course. But the very next afternoon, I got an urgent call from Mike Kaufman to come see him. He was not happy, and it showed. Mike screamed at me and informed me that one of the calculations I had posted on every single page was incorrect. I had apparently reversed the calculation on one of the many formulas used throughout the spreadsheet.

I was horrified by my mistake and wanted to make it up to him. But how? Mike acknowledged that it would probably take me a week to correct the error, and at the same time he also made it clear, in not so kind words, that this would make him late on the list decisions. Mike ended the meeting by telling me to "get it done as soon as possible." It was 6:00 p.m. at the time.

I was still young and very used to pulling all-nighters for my college exams, so that's what I did. I worked all through the night to correct my error and showed up at Mike's door at 9:00 a.m. sharp the very next morning. It's a good thing I was twenty-two years old at the time, as I certainly wouldn't be able to do that today.

I handed Mike the corrected spreadsheets. He looked at me in total disbelief, spot-checked that the calculations were now correct, and then smiled. Mike was highly appreciative of my corrective measures. He didn't ask, but I know he was wondering how I possibly corrected everything that quickly. That's the last time I ever made a mistake with one of my calculations.

I didn't know it at the time, but there were unintended consequences from my timely revisions. The group of Vice Presidents met often, and apparently Mike told them all about my error and miraculous corrections. It was very hard to earn the respect of the very strong-willed management team who could be downright demeaning to us worker bees, but my actions had earned their respect. This became apparent to me a few years later, when I was promoted before some of my peers.

5

They Loved Us

As I wrote in the introduction, I have no doubt that Publishers Clearing House was at one point in time the most loved company in U.S. history. The management at PCH, myself included, relished all the free favorable publicity, which appeared everywhere: on the most well-known daytime and late night talk shows, on many of television's most watched situation comedies, on network and local news, in movie quips, and in magazine and newspaper cartoons. At PCH headquarters, our hallways were lined with many of our favorite cartoons, framed and hung for all to see.

Even one of the first renowned consumer advocates from the 1960's to 1970's, Betty Furness, loved Publishers Clearing House. If you don't know of Betty Furness, she was a model turned movie star turned consumer advocate and news commentator. In one of her commentaries, she fondly said of PCH, "They are the Santa Claus of the magazine business." Her comment referred to the fact that we gave away so much money. But she was also giving us credit for our very generous customer service policies with respect to any and all magazine subscriptions (whether you ordered from us or not).

Let me share some of my favorite PCH references from television and other media.

The Final Episode of Cheers

Few people know this, but three versions were filmed of the final ninety-minute episode of *Cheers*, one of the most popular and beloved television shows of all time. Is there anyone who didn't love that show, which earned 28 Emmy Awards from a then-record 117 nominations? I certainly did. The final episode, which aired on May 20, 1993, achieved one of the largest TV audiences ever, but I don't think that the version the producers and network executives decided to air was very memorable. If you don't remember the final episode, here is a short recap.

Sam Malone (played by Ted Danson) is feeling depressed about his life and continues to go to group therapy when he sees Diane Chambers (played by Shelly Long) on television winning a Cable Award for best writing in a mini-series. Sam decides to get in touch with his former flame, and when he finds out Diane is married, he invites her and her husband to stop by the bar on their next trip to Boston. Sam tells Diane he is also happily married because he suspects that Diane is lying about being married herself. Sam is stunned when Diane shows up with a husband (who is fake), so he enlists the aid of an unhappy and disheveled Rebecca Howe (played by Kirstie Alley) to pose as his wife. When the fake spouses are exposed, Sam and Diane decide they should get married and live in California together.

Sam and Diane are packed and all ready to take off for the West coast, but while waiting for their delayed flight, they realize that spending their lives together would be a big mistake. So Diane goes back to California, alone, and Sam goes back to his true love, his Boston bar.

Woody Boyd (played by Woody Harrelson) embarks on a new life as City Councillor. With help from Woody, beer-drinking Norm Peterson (played by George Wendt) finally gets a job and starts his new life with an accounting firm at City Hall.

And that was pretty much it for the final episode. Not a great way to end that popular show, if you ask me. A much more memorable ending would have been the alternate version that was filmed with the Publishers Clearing House Prize Patrol.

In this alternate ending, the plot for Sam and Diane's reunion and subsequent separation was the same. The added feature, however, was that the PCH Prize Patrol, including the real Dave Sayer and Todd

Sloane, enter Sam Malone's bar – with balloons, champagne, roses, and the big check – to give one of the bar's beloved characters the surprise of his life. The camera catches Woody, the naïve country bumpkin, winning $1 million from Publishers Clearing House.

Below is a photo of Woody's $1 million Big Check from that unaired episode. You can imagine if that version had aired, comedians and newscasters would still be poking fun at Woody and PCH, wondering what Woody is up to these days after becoming a millionaire.

Back at PCH headquarters, Dave proudly displays a picture in his office of him and Todd with the cast of *Cheers* sitting at that infamous bar, "Where everybody knows your name."

Woody's Big Check
Photo from the alternate final episode of Cheers

Conan O'Brien

Apparently, Conan is a big fan of Publishers Clearing House. To promote his new late-night TV show (appropriately named "Conan"), he aired commercials in February 2011 parodying PCH.

The commercial opens with a shot of the Prize Patrol van and several people exiting the van, running towards a house with balloons and flowers. The voice-over announces a familiar PCH line, "Miracles can happen, and dreams do come true."

A shocked and excited woman in curlers opens the door, and Conan, holding a big sign, tells her, "I'm Conan O'Brien, and I'm here to inform you… you can watch Conan at 11 p.m. on TBS."

The woman then realizes it's not the PCH Prize Patrol, and her face falls showing her extreme disappointment.

Jerry Seinfeld

Jerry Seinfeld also liked to have fun with PCH's legendary reputation. In one episode of *Seinfeld* (aired February 18, 1993), Jerry (Jerry Seinfeld), George (Jason Alexander), and Newman (Wayne Knight) have the following interchange:

* George says to Newman, "Let me ask you something. What do you do for a living, Newman?"

* Newman proudly responds, "I'm a United States postal worker."

* George replies sarcastically, "Aren't those the guys that always go crazy and come back with a gun and shoot everybody?"

* Newman, with an evil, mischievous grin, says, "Sometimes."

* Jerry deadpans, "Why is that?"

* Newman then passionately responds, in his infamous ranting and raving style, "Because the mail never stops. It just keeps coming and coming and coming; there's never a let-up. It's relentless. Every day it piles up more and more and more! And you gotta get it out, but the more you get it out, the more it keeps coming in. And then the bar code reader breaks and it's Publisher's Clearing House day!"

The final episode of the *Seinfeld Show* aired in 1998, but that didn't stop Jerry Seinfeld from poking good-hearted fun at Publishers Clearing House just last year. This was in the East Room of the White House on June 2, 2010, when Sir Paul McCartney received the Library of Congress

Gershwin Prize for Popular Song. In addition to live performances by Paul McCartney, Stevie Wonder, Elvis Costello, the Jonas Brothers, and others, Jerry Seinfeld also made an appearance.

In Jerry's White House monologue he quipped: "I also have to say, if I may be completely honest, that I am not that big on prizes. The problem being that the word 'prize' is used to cover just too broad a range of things. You knock over three milk bottles with a baseball, you get a prize…. The Nobel has a prize – I think there's one of them around here somewhere…. Cracker Jacks has a prize. Publishers Clearing House has cash! And prizes."

The celebrities and dignitaries in attendance enjoyed the PCH reference, as we did back home.

In addition to Jerry Seinfeld, other comedians and all the late night talk show hosts were often known to joke about PCH as well.

Jay Leno Monologues

Jay Leno had his own brand of humor in talking about Publishers Clearing House and U.S. Presidents, which he has done on numerous occasions.

My favorite was shortly after President Obama won the Nobel Peace Prize in October 2009. Jay's *Tonight Show* monologue included this joke: "This is President Obama's plan to finance health-care reform. Keep winning these awards – the Nobel, the Powerball, the Publishers Clearing House Sweepstakes – keep winning these, and we can pay for the whole health-care thing."

Saturday Night Live Sketches

SNL sketches also involved Publishers Clearing House, with some very well-known personalities.

One funny parody (aired November 3, 2007) featured Brian Williams, Anchor and Managing Editor of *NBC Nightly News*, along with the *SNL* cast at the time (Kristen Wiig, Fred Armisen, Maya Rudolph, Will Forte, and Amy Poehler).

The spoof showed Kristen Wiig (playing Cheryl) surprising Brian Williams (playing Carl) with a $15 million prize from Publishers Clearing House.

Kristen repeatedly tries to get an emotional reaction out of PCH contest winner Brian, who is totally unresponsive, indifferent, and emotionless. Kristen shows him film clips of other excited winners to try to get him to display some emotion about his big prize, but he is still totally nonchalant about it. Kristen is embarrassed and frustrated by not being able to get the PCH winner excited about his big win. A pizza delivery guy then comes to the door with some "free cheesy bread" with Brian's order. Brian's reaction is immediate. He is finally thrilled and enthusiastic – about the free bread.

In yet another *SNL* spoof (aired January 10, 1998), two famous actors were featured, Samuel L. Jackson and Will Ferrell. In this comedic segment, Samuel L. Jackson plays a poor ghetto dad who unexpectedly wins the Publishers Clearing House sweepstakes.

Late Show with David Letterman

David Letterman loved to poke fun at Publishers Clearing House as well. One especially funny spoof (aired April 8, 1997) featured Ed McMahon, who refuses to get out of the Publishers Clearing House Prize Patrol van. This satire proves again why the myth about where Ed McMahon worked will never die.

Another show (aired January 7, 2002) featured David Letterman himself, who thinks he has a shot at winning the Publishers Clearing House sweepstakes.

Wanda Sykes Show

This relatively new, but short-lived, late night talk show on Fox, hosted by actress and comedian Wanda Sykes, premiered in late 2009. In one skit (aired December 12, 2009), Wanda dresses as white-haired Dave Sayer. Along with two other cast members, they are posing as the Prize Patrol with big million dollar checks for Tiger Woods' mistresses.

The Daily Show with Jon Stewart

This spoof (aired May 16, 2006) was called "Are You Prepared?!?" It featured actress and comedian Samantha Bee playing a correspondent driving up to residential houses and asking the person who answers the door, "Are you prepared?" After getting the door slammed in her face, she changes the sign on her van to read in large bold letters, "Prize Patrol" along with the PCH name and logo. She hopes this will get her more cooperation, but to her consternation, it doesn't.

To Tell The Truth

This long running weekly game show featured Publishers Clearing House not once but twice. In case you don't know this show, it had a panel of four celebrities who tried to guess the real person being featured amongst two imposters.

In the first PCH appearance (in 1991), the show featured our very own Dave Sayer with "Who is Dave Sayer of the Prize Patrol?" Surprisingly, Dave fooled three of the four celebrity panelists.

The second time, several years later, the show featured PCH's favorite millionaire priest with "Who is Father Mike Berner?" Father Mike wasn't able to fool the panel.

Will Smith in *The Fresh Prince of Bel-Air*

In one episode of this NBC sitcom (aired September 20, 1993), Will Smith knocks loudly on the apartment door of his friend Jazz (played by Jeffrey A. Townes). Since Jazz is always in trouble, he won't answer the door. So Will yells, "It's Publishers Clearing House. You've already won!" That gets Jazz to quickly open the door.

Movies

References pertaining to Publishers Clearing House weren't just on television but in the movies as well. Here are a few of the movies that contained funny lines about Publishers Clearing House.

Knight and Day. This 2010 action-comedy film starred Tom Cruise and Cameron Diaz as a fugitive couple racing across the globe during a glamorous and sometimes deadly adventure. Led to believe Roy Knight (played by Tom Cruise) is dead, June (played by Cameron Diaz) follows a clue to a private home in hopes of finding him. She learns the older couple who lives there are Roy's parents, Molly and Frank Knight.

* June asks, "So, uh, you two lived here long?"
* Roy's mom tells June, "This old place? It's been our home for forty years." ... "And we can afford to stay, thanks to Publishers Clearing House."
* June replies, "You won Publishers Clearing House?"
* "Twice," the husband responds.

In the background, there is a picture on the wall of the couple with the big PCH check.

Let's Go to Prison. In this 2006 film, career criminal John Lyshitski (played by actor Dax Shepard) has been in and out of prison his whole life. It all started when at eight years old he tried to carjack the Publishers Clearing House Prize Patrol van, with the real Dave Sayer standing by. He is caught when he tries to cash the giant check and goes into the juvenile system for seven years for his crime.

Top Secret! This 1984 Paramount spoof by the Directors of *Airplane* stars a young twenty-four year old Val Kilmer as Nick Rivers, an Elvis type American heartthrob. In one scene, a mortally wounded spy lies in a dark alley behind the Iron Curtain and is handed an envelope by a frantic woman. She insists it must be postmarked no later than midnight. The envelope is addressed to Publishers Clearing House.

James Patterson Novel

PCH has also found its way into some pretty good novels. A recent (2010) James Patterson bestseller, *Private*, included this line about Publishers Clearing House.

The main character, Jack Morgan, heads the world's most powerful private investigation firm. One of Jack's cases leads him to a dangerous ex-con as he investigates the murder of his best friend's wife. In the book's narrative, Jack relates, "We got out of the fleet car and walked up to the front door of the house. I rang the bell. Rang it again. Then I yelled, 'Open up Perez. You won ten million dollars from the Publishers Clearing House.'"

Cartoons

Lastly, some of the best cartoonists loved to have fun with Publishers Clearing House. Their cartoons referencing PCH have been run in countless newspapers across the country and in dozens of magazines. A small sampling of these follow.

"Non Sequitur" by Wiley Miller
November 9, 2000

"Non Sequitur" by Wiley Miller
March 11, 1993

Good Housekeeping Magazine
May 1989

Newsday: "Pickles"
April 6, 2002

"Oh, all right. I guess we could
stop at *one more* house to 'ask directions'
before we deliver the check."

Newsday: "Close to Home"
April 29, 1997

6   The Key to Our Incredible Success
Testing, Testing, Testing

The Publishers Clearing House sweepstakes were the reason for our notoriety, but it was our massive testing and research program that gave us our incredible success. We called our testing program the lifeblood of our business, and many companies watched and copied what we did. *The New York Times* dubbed PCH a "virtual research factory."

The motivation to test started in the early days of the company and was encouraged by Mr. Mertz himself. One of the first creative geniuses at PCH, Henry Cowen, wrote the following about the early days of testing at PCH in his book, *True Tales of a Junk Mail Whiz*: "We tested all kinds of ideas, looking for ways to improve the profitability of the mail. It was expensive but I was never told not to spend so much money. I was always given a free hand to try anything that might work, and was never second guessed for failures."

Over time, the PCH testing program grew due to the dramatic growth of the business. By the mid-1990's, we were testing an enormous number of new ideas, to the tune of over 200 new promotion elements each year. This included changes in copy, new package formats, product and pricing variations, sweepstakes techniques, and more. Our world-class testing program was a source of great pride, and we evaluated test results very carefully. To our dismay, however, much of what we did was copied by our competitors, the magazine publishers, and the entire direct marketing community. We often complained that many companies didn't do any testing at all but simply watched and copied what we did. And that was, in fact, true.

I was told a funny story about testing in the very early days at PCH. The creative gurus, Henry Cowen, John Mienik, and Bert Rowley, made paper airplanes with the names of their test packages written on them, and then flew them down the long hallways to predict which would win. I can just imagine what this looked like – a bunch of grown men throwing paper airplanes at work, cheering on their own handmade concoctions. This, of course, was just in fun as every new idea was methodically tested before it was rolled out.

In my own beginning at PCH, one of my very first roles was to monitor, evaluate, and report to senior management the results of all test packages. The importance of testing was so ingrained in me that even at the end of my career, in my senior management role, I still carefully monitored test results every week. Over my thirty-year career, I observed thousands of test results relating to everything you could possibly imagine.

Testing

We were often questioned about our mailing packages. This came from friends in general conversation, from our customers through customer contacts, and in our market research studies. The two things people always asked were:

1) Why do you use those annoying lick-em and stick-em magazine stamps, and

2) Why do you make your packages so complicated?

Here is the inside story on those 100 or so annoying little magazine stamps that you have to lick and paste to the order form. We called this component the "stampsheet." The idea for this actually came from another direct marketing company. It was the early 1960's, and a friend of Mr. Mertz who managed Doubleday's Book Club called Harold and told him they were having great success with this new promotional device. Harold had it immediately tested at PCH, and it was a huge success.

Needless to say, the stampsheet has been a fixture in PCH mailings ever since. Over the years, we tried dozens of ways to eliminate this expensive component. There is nothing we would have liked better than to replace it with a less expensive promotional device. However, in the dozens of tests, nothing has ever been as effective as the stampsheet, in spite of its bothersome nature.

Why our mailing pieces are so complicated is another source of constant criticism from both customers and consumers, so we devoted quite a lot of testing to this issue as well. Simplifying the promotion would lower our package cost, so again, we hoped that simpler would be better. Unfortunately, though, every time we tested a simpler promotion versus our standard complicated approach, it just wasn't as effective. Tom Owens, former Senior VP of Creative, said it best when he told a *New York Times* reporter, "We get the best response from messy mailings." At the time, the sweepstakes package contained fourteen components, including fliers, certificates, magazine advertisements, the stampsheet, coupons, and pictures of prizes. To explain why, Tom said, "The longer you have someone looking at what you're trying to sell, the better the odds are they'll make a purchase."

We also knew from our marketing research that consumers don't always tell the truth. In many of our market research studies, respondents who we knew had previously entered our sweepstakes would assert that they never entered contest promotions. Apparently, there are many "closet-enterers" of sweepstakes out there. The same is probably true of the Lottery. We came to realize that we shouldn't believe what consumers say but that we should watch what the consumer does for their real answer.

Out of the thousands of tests worthy of special mention, the strangest was the test of a coffee stain on our general solicitation letter to see if it would add a personal touch to the letter. This did improve results slightly but not enough to pay for itself, so we never rolled it out.

Another test worthy of note because of its special importance was designed to help us with our own internal testing process. At one point our mailings got so very large that even a tiny inaccuracy from the roll-out of a test package could have a multi-million dollar impact on our bottom line… either up or down. At this point in time, we were known for our very scientific approach to testing, and we believed what our statisticians told us. Our test and control panel sizes were larger than at any other direct marketing company, at 100,000 each, and the variability with that panel size was + or –3% according to statistical theory. This meant, for example, that a +2% test result could really be a +5% or a –1%. From a profit standpoint, this was not good news because if we observed a small positive test result, we couldn't really be sure that it wouldn't actually hurt the bottom line. That just wouldn't do! So guess what we did.

We did what we always did when we couldn't answer an important question – we tested it. We carefully designed a set of tests to determine how accurate statistical theory was in real life. We did this by mailing several control panels under the typical random selection in a single promotional campaign (including several other techniques to maintain randomness), and then we evaluated the variability among the control panels. We did this several times in a few mailings with varying outgoing mail volumes.

To our surprise, we found that our testing program, which was based on statistical theory, was faulty. Our conclusion based on this "real life" testing was that we would need to increase test panel size versus what statistical theory indicated or live with the higher variability. This is likely true for all direct mail testing from any company. We surmised that this was probably because of the inherent variability in "real life" postal handling and processing of the mail.

An Unbelievable Test Result – The Power of a Single Word

Out of thousands of tests, one test in particular stands out above all the rest. Normally, in direct mail, and at PCH, a test result that gave a 5% to 10% improvement in sales, or "lift" as it is called, is considered highly successful (after adjusting for any increase or decrease in promotion cost). In fact, most direct mail tests fail and never even beat the standard. Our success rate at PCH was better than most, but still only around one-third, which meant that only one in three tests was successful.

One day one of our tests, with all new copy plus a totally new and unique package format, tested at an extraordinary and unbelievable 100% lift. Not a single person on the management team, including me, believed this shocking test result. To put this into perspective, no other test over my entire thirty-year career even came close to this improvement.

If true, the 100% lift would result in a huge amount of money. But there were two significant problems. First, we didn't know if the result was valid. The result was just too good to be true, so we thought it might be a fluke. Second, due to severe production limitations for the highly unique format, none of our numerous printers could produce the new package format.

At the time we didn't know what aspects of this totally new package were working. All we really knew was that we wanted to, in fact, *had to* roll out this new promotion in our next biggest mailing of the year, our late December TV-supported mailing to around 85 million households.

My particular role at the time had recently shifted to include management of many of the PCH cost centers, and one of these areas included responsibility for all of our print production. This particular department included ten print buyers who managed the work of the dozens of outside printers that we used to manufacture all the components for our mailings. With regard to the new package format, my print production team informed me that none of our print suppliers could rollout the new format. I immediately met with the entire department about this dilemma. I told them they had to find a way to rollout this new promotion, and to go back to every outside printer they knew.

A few weeks later, they all came back with the same answer – no one could handle the unique format we were requesting. Only one printer could do the new format, the printer who had executed the original test. But they couldn't do more than one million packages for our large upcoming mailing. This just wasn't acceptable! I knew that senior management would skin me alive if I told them we couldn't roll out this new package in our large upcoming campaign. And I wouldn't have blamed them. Even if we realized only half of the 100% lift, it would be a stunning result for a single effort.

I knew I had to figure something out. So I met with my two top print managers. One was Tom Bass, who in my opinion is the most knowledgeable print buyer in the world. Tom had been involved in print buying for PCH for over thirty years at the time, and he now managed the department's large staff of print buyers. Tom and his staff were responsible for billions of individual components each year, and that's not an exaggeration. At this point, we were mailing about 350 million packages per year, with seven components in each mailing, which equals 2.5 billion components a year. The other internal print expert at this meeting was Noni Reyes, whose talent was engineering.

Between the two of them, with my guidance and marketing background, and extreme pressure, we found a way to get this done. I informed the senior management team with a large smile on my face that with a relatively minor change to the format we could mail the new promotion to all 85 million consumers in our large upcoming mailing. Mind you, this meant a change in strict company policy, as we never altered a test package when we rolled it out. But I told the Executive team in no uncertain terms that this was the only way to do the new promotion. They agreed to the change.

So not knowing for sure if that fabulous test result would hold up, we rolled out the new copy and unique package format in our largest mailing of the year. It turned out that the mailing was a huge success, and to our surprise and amazement, the 100% lift proved to be completely valid.

But we weren't simply satisfied that the great test result had held up; we wanted to know what was working within the promotion. Was it the new copy? Or was it the unique package format? Or perhaps it was both? So we proceeded to try to find the answer. Over the next several months, we tested a dozen or so versions of the unique format and new copy to isolate what was working. We needed to know what was giving us this stunning result. After evaluating the battery of test results, we concluded that one single word had produced this unprecedented result.

That single powerful word was "Finalist," and there was heated debate by senior management on whether we should use this potent word in our promotions. The copy headline was something like, "*Congratulations, you are a Finalist in the Publishers Clearing House sweepstakes, along with all other timely entrants.*" The official rules defined that all entrants who met the contest deadline were called finalists.

Senior management was split on whether they thought this word was too misleading to use. Some of the management team wanted to use this powerful word (with proper disclosures) in every single mailing to reap the extraordinary rewards in terms of added sales and profit. This was the recommendation of one of our top Vice Presidents. Others thought it was just too misleading, in spite of the qualifying language and explanation in the rules, and thought we shouldn't use it at all.

I knew senior management wouldn't completely walk away from its use, so my recommendation to the management team took a compromise position. I suggested that we use this word sparingly, only a few times a year, with full and proper disclosures. I was overruled, however, and for a short time we proceeded to use this potent word in almost all our mailings. But the heated discussion and decision became moot because in PCH's very first legal agreement with a group of state Attorneys General in 1994, we agreed not to use the word "finalist."

I will confess that to this day, this is one of the few things that I am embarrassed about with respect to management's decisions.

7

My Big Decision

||||||||||||||||||||||||||||||||||||||||||||||||||||||||||||||||||||||||||||||||||||||||||||||||||||||||||||||||||||||||||||||||||||||||||||||||||||

I couldn't rely on any kind of test results for my own big decision. This would be a pure judgment call on my part.

I had been at Publishers Clearing House for almost ten years when I received an unexpected phone call from someone I greatly admired. It was John Mienik, who had recently left PCH after three years at the President's helm. John had taken Lou Kislik's place after Lou abruptly left the nest, and he was now consulting with a competitor, Magazine Marketplace, which was headquartered in the Chicago area. John, of course, knew of my work at PCH and wanted me to jump ship and run Magazine Marketplace as Vice President of Marketing, reporting directly to their President.

I was very intrigued about the opportunity to be a Vice President, which wasn't going to happen anytime soon at PCH. On the other hand, the prospect of leaving my PCH family was unsettling. I loved the PCH environment, my co-workers, and even the bosses, although some could be quite ornery, ill-tempered, and demanding. I had been advancing rapidly with respect to promotions and raises and was now a mid-level Marketing Manager with a medium-sized staff and broad-ranging responsibilities in several areas. My next move would be to Director, and then ultimately to Vice President. However, that level at PCH was a tremendous step up, and at the time, the top level was completely full. Plus, the current group of Vice Presidents were young and didn't look like they were going anywhere any time soon.

PCH had just hired a new President, Robin Smith, who came from Doubleday where she had been President and General Manager of its Dell Publishing subsidiary. Not surprisingly, Robin wasn't well received by the strong personalities of our Vice Presidents, many who wanted to be in the leadership position themselves. It also didn't help that several members of the senior management team were die-hard male chauvinists.

I soon learned that Robin is a remarkably bright and gracious woman. She was one of the first women to graduate with an MBA from Harvard Business School, and her business acumen and accomplishments paved the way for her to serve on the Board of Directors of several large and very prestigious companies. Her most noteworthy Board assignment includes Texaco – one of the largest companies in the world.

Shortly after the call from John, I met with him and the President of Magazine Marketplace in Manhattan. The dinner meeting and interview went extremely well, so the prospect of my leaving PCH became even more likely. We met a second time a few weeks later; they offered me the job on the spot. There would be a very substantial 25% raise plus a fully paid leased car of my choice and that all important title and responsibility of Vice President.

Now I had some hard thinking to do. It was an offer that was too good to pass up. I did some serious soul searching and my wonderful girlfriend at the time, Linda Goor, was very helpful in determining my next step. In the end, I decided to play this one out the only way I knew how – with honesty and integrity.

I reluctantly went to see my boss at PCH, Bruce Pantano, Vice President of Marketing at the time, to inform him of my newfound opportunity. I had worked for Bruce for several years at this point, and I had come to know him as a trustworthy and honorable man. We had an extremely good working relationship, so I was comfortable being completely honest with him. I told Bruce about my phone call from John Mienik, about the offer and raise, and of my strong desire to be a Vice President. I also told Bruce that I hadn't made up my mind yet, and that I didn't really want to leave my PCH family, but that the offer and opportunity as Vice President would be hard to turn down.

I wasn't sure how Bruce or PCH would react to my situation. Whenever this type of thing happened in the past, and it did happen from time to time, PCH did not react kindly – it always ended up with the person being walked out of the building. I certainly didn't want this to happen to me, so I made sure that the tone of my conversation with Bruce was wholly non-threatening. I emphasized my desire to stay at my beloved PCH, and I stressed that I hadn't made up my mind yet. Bruce told me he appreciated my candor and asked that I wait a few days before I did anything so he could discuss my predicament with our new President, Robin Smith.

Two days later, after Bruce talked to Robin, he called me into his office. I still wasn't sure how PCH would handle the situation, but as I said, I knew that prior similar interactions did not end well. Needless to say, I hadn't slept at all the previous few nights.

With a wide smile gracing his face, Bruce told me they had decided to match the offer. He also told me that their counter-offer was something they never do (and I knew that), but that they really wanted me to stay. Bruce said that they would also give me a promotion and more responsibility immediately, in addition to matching the compensation. My new title would be Director, and some additional marketing areas would be put under my control. As to becoming a Vice President at PCH, all Bruce would say was that Robin and he knew that I was VP material and would be a Vice President at PCH some day. They would not, however, tell me when the promotion to VP would happen. I knew that at the present time we were fully staffed at the VP level, and I also knew that at PCH that title was a very dramatic move up in both responsibility and compensation.

So I went back and did more soul searching. I agonized over the decision, making a list of pros and cons. On the one hand, it would be very hard to leave my PCH family, plus management had been so good to me. I loved the atmosphere, camaraderie, and all the people at PCH. In addition, Magazine Marketplace was a much smaller company, only about one-twentieth (or 5%) the size of PCH, so my financial opportunities might be limited.

On the other hand, however, I could use everything that I had learned at PCH to help Magazine Marketplace grow. And most importantly, getting the title of Vice President and fully running the show was extremely enticing. If I accepted the job, I would work from their Manhattan office and would travel to the Chicago area once a month or so.

It was a very difficult decision, and it was a close call, but I decided to stay at PCH. I told Bruce and Robin I would stay, but I voiced my disappointment about not being given a stated time frame for becoming Vice President.

With my decision made, I now had to make two phone calls. I dreaded making the call to inform the President of Magazine Marketplace, but I knew I had to phone John Mienik first, and this would be an even more difficult call to make.

I really feared calling John; he had been so supportive and hopeful that I would make the move. Also, because of John's charismatic nature and the fact that everyone knew him as a creative genius, he was not somebody you generally said no to. I forced myself to make this call. To my relief, John took the news very professionally and said he understood.

Timing is everything. A few months later, there was a surprise announcement at PCH. Two of our Vice Presidents, Steve Stark and Jerry Reitman, were leaving. The ranks of Vice President were now wide open, especially since Steve was Senior VP of Marketing. My day would come sooner rather than later.

8   The First PCH Scandal

Arnold Diaz

Many years after my big decision, PCH had its own big decision to make... how to handle the first ever negative news directed at PCH.

After years of admiration, accolades, and good natured humor thrown our way, we experienced our first criticism. The very first negative news story about Publishers Clearing House came from Arnold Diaz back in 1992, and his harmful story was all over the news. Mr. Diaz was a novice news reporter at the time, and I often think that PCH gave him his start. He later became a winner of 36 Emmy Awards for his consumer investigative reporting and was known for regularly exposing wrongdoing and incompetence by private industry and government agencies. Some of his reporting has even led to new legislation or jail time for his victims.

It was the fall of 1992, and it began when some city sanitation workers in Queens found some sweepstakes envelopes from Publishers Clearing House discarded by the roadside. The sanitation workers called investigative consumer reporter Arnold Diaz of WCBS-TV, who then put PCH in the news. His news report, to our surprise, implied that Publishers Clearing House routinely discarded our sweepstakes entries. The PCH management team, including me, was horrified about the negative media coverage. We had never had anything but good publicity before, and we had no idea how to handle the situation. We were worried that the negative publicity would tarnish our good name; we were, of course, also concerned that it would have a disastrous effect on our results.

The negative news coverage appeared everywhere and hit at an exceptionally bad time. All our senior executives were heading off to Dallas, Texas for a lavish party we were hosting to celebrate PCH's 25th anniversary of awarding prizes. Many previous prize winners from around the country were invited in addition to numerous friends, suppliers, clients, and business colleagues in the direct marketing community. No one at PCH wanted to miss the festive occasion.

Bruce Pantano, Executive Vice President at the time, and I volunteered to stay behind. Bruce would be the point person for all the negative publicity, and I would assist him however possible.

We fully investigated what happened and then tried to explain it to Mr. Diaz and the rest of the press. Upon examination, we determined that 2,180 entries had been dumped in Queens; approximately 95% were non-orders and 5% were orders. Our investigation also uncovered that the discarded entries were the result of one dissatisfied worker from a supplier that helped us process our mail. We never found out the reason for the worker's discontent or why he tossed our unprocessed mail onto the side of the road, but this single incident caused all the controversy.

We explained that the discarded PCH entries were just a simple mistake by a single individual, and that we absolutely do not throw away our sweepstakes entries until after they are processed. To our chagrin, however, Arnold Diaz and the other news outlets didn't believe us. The sad fact was that the press was not at all interested in our explanation as to what had happened. It soon became clear to PCH management that Mr. Diaz and his staff wanted to vilify PCH.

The negative press continued when a New Jersey man saw the Arnold Diaz report, and fearing that his entry was among the discarded entries, he sued PCH. For the life of us, we couldn't understand why no one believed our explanation or the hard fact that the entries found discarded also contained orders. But the news reports kept implying the same thing – that PCH threw out its sweeps entries. The press conveniently left out of their reporting that orders had also been found discarded.

The fact of the matter was that the massive quantity of incoming orders and non-orders we received was becoming more and more difficult to handle. I would describe the process at PCH during the peak periods as "highly organized chaos." We didn't have the space nor the manpower to process the vast volume of mail. Because of this situation, we needed three sources of extra help to process all the orders and non-orders. This included considerable part-time help at our Port Washington headquarters, the use of several outside suppliers who had their own staff, and the use of what we called "home workers." These "home workers" were individuals who helped PCH process the orders and non-orders we received, but they did this work at their homes. Most home workers were local moms with young children who appreciated being able to work from home and earn some extra money, and we thought this was a great thing to do for the community and the surrounding areas.

In order to appease the press, we announced that we would tighten our quality controls and discontinue use of any outside suppliers that we couldn't directly supervise. In addition, so as not to fire all the local home worker moms, we decided that until things calmed down all home workers had to do their work at PCH headquarters.

Also, to settle the lawsuit, we agreed to enter all the names and addresses of everyone who received mailings from us between February 1992 to October 1992 into our $10 million contest, whether the consumer had returned the entry or not. If only all our subsequent lawsuits could have been settled so easily.

A few months later, during our peak season in mid-January 1993, Arnold Diaz once again reported negative news about PCH. This time he said he was disappointed that a Long Island firm called Eastern Mail and Data was handling Publishers Clearing House sweepstakes mail. Mr. Diaz chastised PCH by saying, "I think they've gone back on their word," and that, "We're trying to hold their feet to the fire." We explained that, in this particular case, the outside supplier was only handling mail that our computers couldn't process like change of address transactions. However, we also found out that this supplier was using home workers, which violated our contract with them, so we terminated the use of that supplier.

Believe it or not, during the media frenzy about PCH mail processing, we found the press actually looking through the garbage cans at PCH headquarters to see if they could find any more discarded contest entries. Who knows what the media would have said if they had found just one more batch of discarded sweeps entries, whether they were already processed or not? It got so bad that we had to have our maintenance crew guard our trash bins.

Disconcerting though this all was, the situation did teach me a valuable lesson about the press. What seemed to matter most to Mr. Diaz and the rest of the news media was how to get the best headlines and best ratings, not the facts. I am sorry to say that it taught me never to believe what you read or hear in the news.

The most ironic part of this story, which we didn't realize for several months, was that our sales actually increased following this controversy and our induction into the Arnold Diaz Hall of Shame. We had been expecting the negative publicity to result in lower sales, so we monitored results carefully for the ensuing months. To our surprise, the negative media coverage, which as I said, horrified senior management, actually resulted in better results for PCH. Can you guess why?

Apparently, the media coverage reinforced the common mistaken belief that to win the contest you had to place an order. The unintentional end result was that during this period consumers ordered more than usual from us. I guess there is truth in the statement that negative publicity can be good! I don't think Arnold Diaz knows that his reporting actually improved our results. If you see him, please don't say anything to him. I don't think that will make him happy.

9

The Roller Coaster Ride Up

The Good Times at PCH

At this point in my story, I would like to chronicle the five decades of amazing growth at PCH.

For almost half a century, from our very first day in 1953 when Harold Mertz mailed out 10,000 envelopes from his Long Island home until the late 1990's, Publishers Clearing House realized phenomenal growth. For this long stretch of time, sales and profits grew virtually every year – by 10%, 20%, 30%, or more. That kind of growth for almost five decades is quite remarkable.

Over time, PCH became viewed by our peers in the publishing and direct marketing communities as true leaders and, in fact, business colleagues and competitors called Publishers Clearing House "the gold standard." And by the 1990's, our sweepstakes and marketing strategies were being copied by hundreds of companies worldwide.

PCH's success reached a level that no one, not Harold Mertz, nor the management team, thought was possible. At one point, our Treasurer compared PCH's profitability to what appeared in *Forbes* ranking of the largest 500 private companies in the United States. By his account, our profits at the time would rank PCH in the top twenty to twenty-five out of all private companies in the country. Interestingly, almost all of these top companies had many thousands of employees compared to PCH's mere 600 employees.

Harold Mertz's guiding principles of unwavering attention to detail, open mindedness, and belief in testing were the underlying reasons for our exceptional success. More specifically, the following promotional and marketing factors contributed to our growth through the years:

- Lowest magazine price guarantee (1953).

- Cultivation and growth of a customer file (1950's and '60's).

- Sweepstakes start (1967).

- Newly added promotional ideas and copy (1960's) – Stampsheet, One-Quarter Part Pay option, etc.

- Personalization (1970's) – Variable copy in the direct mail packages tailored to the individual consumer.

- Television advertising (mid-1970's).

- Statistical modeling (late 1970's) – Statistical regression techniques to improve customer selections.

- Merchandise (mid-1980's) – Introduction of a wide range of merchandise including home entertainment products like books, videos, and music, household and personal items, horticulture, food, and collectibles.

- Bigger top prize (mid-1980's).

- More aggressive direct mail copy and marketing tactics, along with added mailings (mid to late 1980's).

- Birth of the Prize Patrol (1988).

- First "live" Super Bowl winner and commercial (1995).

The 1950's and 1960's

Most of this book so far has discussed these early years, so I won't recap those here except to repeat that the fundamental policies that Harold Mertz put in place plus instituting sweepstakes were probably the most important ingredients to the young and growing Publishers Clearing House.

The 1970's

When I started at PCH in 1973, the management and owners were delighted with the company's strong growth and track record. At the time, PCH sales were about $75 million a year and growing, and we were very profitable. PCH was still a relatively small mom and pop company, with less than 150 employees, most of whom were clerical, operational, and support staff. I was hired as an entry level Marketing Analyst, and I was learning the business from the best talent around.

In these early days, we took a very scientific, controlled, and cautious approach to everything we did. We never changed or altered any of our direct mail packages, not a single word or color, unless it was fully tested and reported upon. The PCH testing and research programs were getting bigger and bigger, and we were becoming known as a great direct marketing innovator.

The business model that Harold Mertz had founded was working brilliantly; plus, there was absolutely no competition. This model was helped by our strict policy of only paying the magazine publishers a commission (or "remit" as we called it) of merely 5% to 10% of the magazine subscription price. This meant that when PCH sold a magazine subscription for $10.00, PCH kept $9.00 to $9.50, and the magazine publisher received only 50 cents to $1.00. This was viable for the publisher because PCH paid all the costs of getting the new subscriber while the publisher made most of their revenue from the advertising in the magazine itself. Many magazines would come to rely heavily on the new subscriptions PCH produced, and these new subs became a foundation for many publishers' entire circulation planning. In addition, no publisher wanted to miss its circulation number, or rate base, as it was called. This was the number of consumers reading a particular magazine and was used as the basis for the fee advertisers charged. If a publisher missed its circulation number, it would be very costly when advertisers sought some form of refund for circulation not delivered.

As you can imagine, this low magazine commission structure created a very favorable situation for PCH's profitability. And in spite of the meager commission, nearly every major publisher in the United States, representing over 350 magazines, was promoted in a PCH mailing at some point in time. Also working in our favor was that we promoted only 100 to 120 magazines in any given mailing, so the publishers fought to get into the PCH mailing program. To our delight, many publishers even started offering attractive free premiums with their magazine subscriptions in order to be featured in our mailings. That made our magazine offers to the consumer even more attractive.

Stew Eisberg, a circulation expert with over thirty years experience, including many years at *Newsweek*, summed up the publishers' eagerness for new subscriptions from PCH in *Folio*, a trade publication: "They're risk-free. If we mail one million names and get no response, we still have to pay for the mailing. If Publishers Clearing House does the mailing, we don't pay for anything." His point was that in every industry, companies pay a lot of money to bring in new customers, but the PCH model was a completely risk-free way to attain those sought after new customers.

PCH's phenomenal growth continued through the 1970's, and I was continuing to grow as well. During this decade I worked long hours and learned every aspect of the business. During the next decade, I rose up through the ranks of the Marketing department, from Manager to Director to Assistant Vice President.

The 1980's – A Competitor Wakes The Sleeping Giant

The decade of the 1980's started off quite well for PCH, and we continued to prosper and grow.

Our relationship with the publishers, however, was strained, and within the confines of the walls at PCH, we would talk about the love-hate relationship PCH had with our magazine clients. On the one hand, the publishers loved and needed the new subscriptions PCH was producing. But it was almost like a narcotic. The more subs we gave them, the more they wanted and needed. On the other hand, however, the magazine publishers despised the arrogant way they were treated by PCH management. Sadly, this was of no concern to the PCH top brass, and that turned out to be a big mistake.

Over the years, the PCH management team laughed at any new multi-magazine competitor trying to enter the field that we completely dominated. Many had tried and failed miserably, including several large publishers. This, I am sure, contributed to the PCH arrogance.

The latest newcomer and competitor in our marketplace, American Family Publishers, was founded a few years earlier in 1977. The story I am told is that the PCH bosses were being their typical arrogant selves in dealing with our largest publishing client, Time Inc. At a meeting with senior management from both companies, Time Inc. again requested that their well-known titles (*Time, People, Sports Illustrated, Fortune,* and *Money*) receive a higher commission than the paltry 5% to 10% they had been receiving. Although these titles were generally among the best sellers in our mailings, PCH management continued to show its condescending side. Time Inc. management was again told "no" to their request... in not so nice words. It was at this very moment that a new competitor was born.

The management at Time Inc. didn't like the answer we gave them, but more than that, they were furious about how they were being treated. There wasn't much they could do, however, because they needed the new subscriptions PCH was producing for them. So Time Inc. management went home, joined forces with two other major publishers, and put together a plan to start up a new competitor called American Family Publishers.

The original founders of AFP were Time Inc., Meredith Corp., and McCalls Corp. However, shortly before the new venture even got off the ground, Meredith got cold feet and backed out. That left Time Inc. and McCalls Corp., but even with this early setback, their resources were unlimited. Time Inc. was the largest magazine publisher in the world, and McCalls Corp. was owned by the Pritzker family, one of the wealthiest families in America. The Pritzkers were owners of the Hyatt Hotel chain, a major airline, and scores of other large, important businesses.

The parent companies of American Family Publishers had extraordinarily deep pockets and the intense desire to give the cocky and insolent PCH a run for their money. Because of the unlimited resources, some of our management team and owners were concerned. However, despite AFP's entry into the marketplace in 1977, we continued to prosper and grow through the early 1980's. We were very pleased that we could accomplish this, in spite of the new competitor. At this point, there were mixed opinions on how much a threat AFP was to our business. Both PCH and AFP were offering similar top prizes of $200,000 to $250,000 at the time.

Then in 1982 everything changed. American Family Publishers started to get very aggressive with their marketing and creative efforts. AFP's tactics included the introduction of a well-known and respected spokesman, Ed McMahon. In addition, AFP increased their top prize to $1 million, and also started to do massive amounts of television advertising. This caught PCH by complete surprise, and of special concern was AFP's increase in their top prize amount. The deep pockets of AFP's two wealthy owners were starting to show.

Over the next few years AFP upped the stakes even more and pulled off more big surprises. AFP increased their top prize a second time, this time to $2 million in 1983, and then again to $10 million in 1984.

For the first time ever PCH profits declined, and it was a rude awakening to the PCH management team and our owners. After decades of consistent double-digit growth, we were stunned by the profit decline. I recall there were lots of senior management meetings on what to do. After considerable internal discussion, it was decided that we would allocate a large amount of money to try to combat our competitor's aggressive tactics. We called this our "war chest."

We also debated how to counter AFP's aggressive promotions. At first, we were reluctant to follow AFP's lead and increase our top prize. We considered all our options, and even discussed whether to promote a bigger prize than AFP's $10 million prize. However, we speculated that the deep-pocketed AFP would simply match whatever we did, and the end result would be ever increasing top prizes. We felt that nobody would win that game, and it would just produce higher costs. In the end, we felt we had no choice, so we matched AFP's top contest amount of $10 million. We hoped that AFP wouldn't go any higher; luckily, they didn't.

We also tapped into our enormous testing and research programs, and started to get more aggressive with our marketing and creative efforts. Around this time, in 1986, the Pritzkers sold *McCalls* magazine but retained their 50% share in American Family Publishers, which indicated their desire to invest in the growth of AFP.

Back at PCH, we also considered hiring a spokesperson to combat AFP's use of Ed McMahon and subsequent use of Dick Clark. We researched several familiar and respected celebrities of the day. Now remember, this was the 1980's. Our short list included Pat Boone (well-known singer, actor, and writer), Ed Asner (from *The Mary Tyler Moore Show* and *Lou Grant* television series), and Eva Gabor (actress of *Green Acres* fame and Zsa Zsa Gabor's sister). Our first choice was Ed Asner, but he wanted way too much money. So we decided on Eva Gabor, and in 1987 we tested her as our spokesperson. We filmed some very interesting commercials with Ms. Gabor in a bathtub with lots of soapy bubbles. However, I guess sex appeal doesn't always sell because the results were unimpressive. We concluded that our name, Publishers Clearing House, was already so well-known that having an expensive spokesperson wasn't the way to go.

In hindsight, having those two distinguished spokesmen was a very successful strategy for AFP. It gave them instant credibility against a competitor, PCH, who owned the marketplace at the time. At one point, we heard rumors that Ed McMahon and Dick Clark might be replaced by Dolly Parton. On hearing this, we kept our sense of humor and joked, "That would be replacing two boobs with two bigger boobs."

Within just a few years of AFP's aggressiveness, by the late 1980's, thanks to our extensive testing and research programs, PCH profits were back on track and increasing at a very fast pace. Our new-found growth was due to several factors, including our new $10 million top prize, expanded promotion of merchandise items, better television advertising by surprising our contest winners via the innovative Prize Patrol, additional mailings to our customers, and more aggressive direct mail copy and marketing.

The PCH management team and owners were pleased we could get our growth back on the fast track, especially in face of AFP's aggressive tactics.

The 1990's

This is the decade where PCH hit its stride and two new milestones were reached. In 1990, PCH sales and profit reached an impressive new high point… $500 million in annual sales. At that time, I, too, reached my own personal milestone as I became Vice President of Marketing and became an Officer of the company.

The PCH management team, myself included, felt that our new high sales level was an impressive feat since it was accomplished at the same time we had an aggressive and wealthy competitor at our throat. Even our own industry's trade organization, the Direct Marketing Association, recognized PCH for yet a second time; Robin Smith, our Chairwoman, was honored in 1991 with their Marketer of the Year Award. And on top of that, there were some large, respected companies that wanted to buy PCH. One of the most interesting parties, at least according to rumors, was Readers Digest. That would have made a fascinating pairing. But the Mertz family had no interest in selling their company and wouldn't even listen to the offer.

The workload by now was getting seriously out of control. Our accelerated growth in sales, number of mailings, and tests were not matched by staff increases. We had about 525 full-time employees in 1990, but that was nowhere near enough to handle the increased workload, so we went on a hiring binge to be able to handle and manage the exponentially increasing amount of work. In true PCH style, we were still doing full detailed reports on every test and every mailing.

Then in 1992, the totally unexpected happened. Sales had just previously reached the staggering milestone of $500 million per year when sales increased again – by a stunning 100% from what they were just the previous year. All of a sudden, we reached another new milestone, one that no one ever imagined… $1 billion in annual sales!

PCH management felt that for a business that had started in Harold Mertz's basement, this was pretty damn good. The new sales milestone was due to a combination of great marketing and creative ideas that came out of our extensive testing program. We had trouble handling the growth before this explosion, but now things got even busier. All companies should face this kind of problem.

We stayed at around $1 billion in annual sales from 1992 through 1998, and it took us several years to staff up to handle the dramatically higher workload. We eventually doubled the PCH staff size and grew to over 1,000 full-time employees. All in all, despite our growth challenges, life at PCH was grand. The long roller coaster ride up was fantastic fun, and I felt lucky to have been an integral part of it. In fact, during this period (in 1996), I reached my own career pinnacle when I became a Senior Vice President.

At this point in time, many companies were following PCH's lead. By the mid to late 1990's, there were several multi-magazine agencies competing with us, plus approximately 300 other companies using a direct mail sweepstakes. Almost everyone, including numerous publishers and other direct marketing firms, were taking advantage of PCH's enormous testing program and copying what we did. It didn't help that a trade publication, *Advertising Age*, reported what PCH had known for years – that direct marketers could increase sales by an astounding 50% or more through sweepstakes.

Just how large PCH had become and how immense our mailing program had gotten is evidenced by the following few facts:

1) PCH's mail volume reached 500 million a year. Our single largest mailing in January went to over 85 million households. At the time, there were about 95 million households in the U.S., so our largest single mailing was reaching almost 90% of all American homes.

2) We estimated that PCH was printing more individual stamps on our stampsheet, counting the individual stamps for each magazine and product offer, than postage stamps being printed by the United States Postal Service.

3) At a local celebration in Port Washington for PCH's 50th anniversary, Executive Vice President Debbie Holland put PCH's size into perspective. She was quoted as saying, "The number of pieces of mail is over 10 billion, so I guess that puts us up there with the number of McDonald's hamburgers sold."

Any company that grew as fast as we did would experience growing pains, and two of ours are worth noting. Our biggest problem was the internal process that we used to create all the components in the numerous mailings. The second challenge (although not as problematic with respect to the bottom line impact) was the space to house all the new employees plus the room needed to store and process the unprecedented amount of incoming mail.

THE BRICK WALL: The first challenge was brought about by the colossal increase in the number of mailings each month. Despite the increased manpower, our internal process to create the unique, individual components was about to implode under its own weight. At the time, 1996, I realized we were going to hit a brick wall.

As mentioned previously, a few years earlier my job responsibilities had changed. I was now managing many of the cost centers at PCH, including all the areas that handled and controlled the printing of our packages. Because our growth had been so great the previous several years, most of our cost centers were completely out of control. We knew this, and that was partly the reason I was put in charge of these areas.

The unbelievable growth in number of mailings plus the goal of having a different promotion, or package, for each mailing, along with tons of new test packages, finally became too much to handle. At this point in time, we had three mailings each week – which is a mailing almost every other day. And in addition, most mailings included a set of test packages. Based on all of this increased activity, for just one month's time, there would be several hundred unique components which needed copy written, multiple layers of review and approval by our legal team and by senior management, photographs to be shot for the merchandise we sold, cover art obtained for the magazine covers, all files prepped for live production, and much more. Part of the problem was that the internal process we used was the same as when we were a small business, and part was because staff increases couldn't keep pace with the increasing workload.

To control this massive activity, I had asked one of my new departments, called the "Traffic" department, to put together a weekly summary of the workload status for the upcoming few months. This report would count every component in our numerous upcoming mailings and would also indicate the status of each component. This was relatively easy to document because the information was already logged into the computer. It was just a matter of summarizing the data by week. I met with my department heads weekly to review this new information. Shortly after I initiated this task, the data indicated that almost three-quarters of the hundreds of components were running late. Due to the increasing workload leading up to our peak mailing period at year-end, this meant we would never be able to catch up.

I determined that the only thing that would get us back on track was to immediately institute mandatory overtime and weekend work, plus hiring additional temporary professionals to help. I did this in my departments, but I needed the Creative department, which didn't report to me, to do the same. I met with Vic Zolfo, Creative VP at the time, but he didn't believe my assessment of the situation. Vic told me that none of the overtime measures I suggested were needed, especially since his staff was already working really hard. I had to try not to laugh at his response, especially since it was no laughing matter. I knew his staff wasn't putting in any extra time, and that if something wasn't done immediately, it would be like a house of cards crashing down.

Since Vic wouldn't agree to my suggested overtime for his department, I had no choice but to inform my boss, Executive VP Bruce Pantano, and our President, Robin Smith, about the situation. After I explained the problem to them, they agreed to talk to Vic. I wasn't at the meeting they had, but apparently Vic convinced them that the situation wasn't that dire.

Two weeks later things got even worse. This time I called an emergency meeting with all the parties involved – myself, Vic, Bruce, and Robin. At this meeting, Vic finally recognized there was a serious problem and agreed to institute mandatory overtime and weekend work for his large creative staff. We also agreed to meet again as a group in a few weeks to discuss our progress.

A few weeks later, after I checked how we were doing, we all met again. I informed the trio that the overtime was too little, too late, and

I advised them that we had to do something drastic, or dozens of mailings and tests would go out late. They all knew that if this happened, it would be a disaster because these mailings were all being supported by our very expensive television campaign. To make matters worse, late mail would also mean that consumers wouldn't be able to respond in time to meet the short contest deadlines which would most certainly kill our response rates. These deadlines couldn't change because they were all tied into the ending date of the registered contest on Super Bowl Sunday. All in all, this was a very major problem.

At this meeting, I suggested the unthinkable. I recommended that we cancel all tests for a two month period. The workload would then be reduced, which would hopefully allow the many large standard mailings to go out on time. The top brass agreed, and for the first time in PCH history, we canceled all tests. In spite of continued overtime the next several weeks and the cancelled tests, we couldn't salvage everything.

The bottom line was that we ended up having several late mailings for the first time ever. It could have been much worse though. When we totaled it all up, the damage was several million dollars less profit for that time period. I don't really blame myself for this, but I wish I could have been more persuasive earlier on.

Over the next few years, I raised the red flag again every once in a while for the same problem, and we were always proactive enough, even in the Creative department, to overcome the situation.

LACK OF SPACE: With respect to the second challenge, we were hiring so many people to handle the new workload that there was just no more room left. This was in spite of the fact that just a few years earlier we had prepared for our growth needs by constructing a brand new, three-story building next door to our Port Washington headquarters. But both buildings were now fully occupied, so we considered putting a second floor on our one-story Port Washington facility. The engineers, however, advised us this would not be a good idea. Our headquarters had been built on an abandoned sand pit, so the underlying ground would not support the weight of a second story. We were told that if we put up a second floor, the first floor would soon become the basement.

Our space problem got so bad that we actually had fights over closet space. I am pretty much a pacifist, but space was such a cherished commodity that one afternoon I found myself having a rather fierce argument with another VP to give me their closet space to house some of my new employees.

After many internal battles over where to put the new hires, in 1993, we finally resolved the problem by leasing 235,000 square feet in a building about thirty minutes away in Syosset, New York.

The End of the Ride Up (1999)

As I have said, despite these growth problems, riding the roller coaster up with respect to sales and profits was tremendous fun in spite of the long hours and hard work. But in 1999, as we had finally fully staffed up, everything changed yet again, and again the totally unexpected happened. But this time, it was not good news. Virtually overnight, results took a dramatic nosedive.

It was as if we had reached the pinnacle of a very long upward roller coaster ride, and then the roller coaster took its sharp plunge down. Sales dropped by 50%. Profits were not just down, but in the red, and turmoil took over.

10   The Firestorm of Negative Press

We were totally unprepared for what happened in early 1999 when the bottom dropped out. The devastation occurred not just at PCH but for the entire direct marketing industry as well. Here is how it all started and a sampling of how bad it got.

It all began in late 1997, when an elderly consumer flew five hours to collect his millions from our major competitor, American Family Publishers. This single incident turned the tides against an entire industry, and ignited an avalanche of negative publicity and lawsuits. For PCH in particular, the negative media coverage fueled the lawsuits against us, and the ensuing lawsuits then fueled the negative press. They fed on each other, like gasoline on a fire.

The event that triggered the outcry occurred when our overly aggressive competitor, AFP, mailed a promotion with the following headline: *"It's down to a 2 person race for $11,000,000 -- You and one other person were issued the winning number."* This deceptively worded promotion prompted eighty-eight year old Richard Lusk to take the long journey from his southern California home to Tampa, Florida, where AFP's Customer Service Center was located. Mr. Lusk was convinced that his previous winning entries had been lost in the mail, so this time he went in person to collect his millions.

This was, in fact, the second time Richard Lusk flew to Tampa to collect his prize. Four months earlier, Mr. Lusk had flown to Tampa with his very reluctant sixty-three year old son, who had tried unsuccessfully to convince his dad not to take the long journey. Try as he might, his dad just wouldn't listen to reason. He first tried by reading his dad the fine print that stated, *"Any entrant that comes in person to collect their winnings will be automatically disqualified."* But that didn't work, so he tried by telling his dad that the odds of winning were hundreds of million to one. This also didn't work, so the only thing Richard Lusk's son could do was to fly to Florida along with his elderly father. Both were treated poorly and disrespectfully by the Tampa Customer Service Center who laughed at them behind their backs. The day after returning home from their cross-country odyssey, the elderly Richard Lusk suffered a stroke.

Four months later, in December 1997, Richard Lusk went on a similar mission. But this time, he avoided telling his son and flew off without his son's knowledge. When Mr. Lusk's son learned his dad was in Tampa, he was concerned that something bad might happen to his confused and elderly father, so he alerted the Tampa police, the airport police, the news media, and officials from AFP. Richard Lusk again came home empty-handed, but not before a whole lot of media attention. Later on, his family and the entire world discovered that Richard Lusk had a secret. He was addicted to entering direct mail sweepstakes, privately entering and buying from everyone. It was reported that he spent at least $50,000 over five years on magazine subscriptions, products, and charitable donations with dozens of sweepstakes mailers including AFP, PCH, Readers Digest, Time Inc., Easter Seals, the National Children's Cancer Society, and others. Richard Lusk said that he wasn't looking for a lifetime of luxury; he just wanted to make sure there was enough money to take care of his wife of sixty-five years who was bedridden. Media coverage of this incident and Richard Lusk's situation was all over the news.

As bad as this was, however, it was not an isolated incident. All totaled, about twenty-five people flew to Tampa to collect their millions from AFP. Another example was George Lum, another elderly gentleman at seventy-eight. He wrote each of his five children a check for $1 million and flew through six time zones from his home in Honolulu. Like Mr. Lusk, Mr. Lum believed the only way to collect his winnings was to show up in person. Mr. Lum explained that he tried calling and writing AFP first, but to no avail; he then lied to his ailing wife about where he was going, saying he was "visiting a friend in Virginia," and wrote to his children that he hoped the prize money would heal a family rift.

The situation at AFP's Customer Service Center became so disconcerting to the customer service manager for the sweepstakes account, Anne E. Curran, that she filed a lawsuit against AFP. The suit stated, "The individuals Curran met with who had traveled to Tampa to claim prizes they believed they had won in the A.F.P. sweepstakes were often very angry or very depressed upon learning that they had not won and had traveled to Tampa for nothing." The suit went on to claim, "As a consequence, Curran began to experience emotional distress and fear for her personal safety." The lawsuit also reported that so many individuals came that they were given the code name "visitors," and Ms. Curran was instructed to keep cash in a fund "specifically set up to silence them."

Meanwhile, AFP tried to make amends with Richard Lusk and his family. They sent Richard Lusk's son a letter of apology along with a check for $1,930 to cover their travel costs to Florida, and also issued a refund on his father's magazine subscriptions. Clearly, this was insufficient in addressing the trauma to the Lusk family.

Back at PCH, the management team, including me, was shocked and distraught to see that most of the negative press was directed at Publishers Clearing House, especially since AFP was the main culprit. This misdirected publicity occurred for two reasons: First, PCH was the most recognizable name and leader in the field, and, second, because neither the press nor the consumer could tell the difference between AFP and PCH.

In addition to the reporting of the Richard Lusk saga, all three major TV networks, ABC, NBC, and CBS, started showing heart-breaking images of elderly, distraught sweeps entrants surrounded by weeping relatives amid stacks of magazines and unopened packages. The press couldn't get enough of these heart-wrenching stories as the images made poignant TV news. The stories went on to report how these trusting souls had spent their entire life savings on magazines and products from all the sweepstakes mailers. Negative stories about PCH and AFP filled the airways from morning until night, including *60 Minutes, Dateline,* all the network evening news stations, and all the morning talk shows. The harsh and damaging news reports almost always included Publishers Clearing House in their stories.

Besides television's constant negative news reports, critical stories also ran in virtually every major newspaper across the country and on into Canada, including *The New York Times, Chicago Tribune, The Wall Street Journal, USA Today, Long Island Newsday, The Miami Herald, The International Herald Tribune, The Toronto Star,* and more. Negative magazine articles abounded as well, including *Consumer Reports, Newsweek,* and our own industry trade publications. Even the esteemed AARP joined in with anti-PCH articles in several of their bulletins. And to top it all off, renowned columnist Ann Landers, with 90 million readers in more than 1,200 newspapers, joined the bandwagon and chastised the sweepstakes marketers in her columns. All of the harsh negative press was very unsettling to the PCH management team.

The promotion by American Family Publishers that triggered the avalanche of negative media coverage, in my opinion, was clearly deceptive. AFP must have been aware of the problem; otherwise, they wouldn't have included the line in their rules about disqualifying consumers who tried to enter the sweeps in person. Still, I can't but wonder how AFP's legal team allowed this promotion to go out. A source who worked at AFP informed me that their lawyers were pressured to allow it through by Susan Caughman, the CEO of AFP at the time. However, Ms. Caughman, in turn, blamed the lawyers. I believe both should have taken responsibility for this suspect promotion.

I could fill an entire book recounting all the negative news stories, headlines, bulletins, and statements about PCH. I will spare you that… I had to live through it once already. But to help give you a better understanding of the situation, I will share three examples of the kind of negative publicity we had to endure.

The first example concerns the Attorney General of Wisconsin, Jim Doyle. PCH was being sued by most of the states, and the lawsuit by the state of Wisconsin against PCH was in the pre-trial stage. Although it is highly inappropriate to make negative remarks to the press during a trial, Attorney General Jim Doyle did so anyway. He called us "**burglars**" and said there was a "**special place in hell**" for PCH. These negative and inflammatory remarks were, of course, published in *Newsday*, reported on NBC's *Dateline* and countless other media outlets. Afterwards, Mr. Doyle defended his comments by saying he intended to continue doing his job by warning people about problems he saw in his state.

It should be noted that Mr. Doyle had previously announced plans to run for Governor, and even the press reported that his highly visible attacks on PCH were probably politically motivated. Mr. Doyle's remarks were totally unfair, as even the impartial Wisconsin state judge in the case indicated that to be the case. This judge, citing his responsibility to supervise the litigation in a way that's fair to all parties, said he found Doyle's statements "troubling" because of the impact they might have on the public. Predictably, the negative comments by the Attorney General of Wisconsin were widely reported in the media while the judge's rebuke got absolutely no media attention at all. Mr. Doyle subsequently won the seat for Governor of Wisconsin.

The next two examples do not refer directly to Publishers Clearing House, but as I wrote earlier, any negative news about sweepstakes was thought by the consumer to be an attack aimed at Publishers Clearing House.

This example is from a reader who wrote to columnist Ann Landers and is actually a reference to the aforementioned Richard Lusk in the AFP incident. Ann Landers' headline in her column on March 26, 1998, declared, "**Sweepstakes Misleading.**" In this much-read column, the following letter was printed for millions to see: "*Dear Ann Landers: I recently saw a story and photo that moved me to tears. It showed a white-haired gentleman, age 88, weeping with his son looking on. It seems the man boarded a plane for Tampa, clutching a letter that carried a five-day deadline. It read, 'Final results are in, and they're official. You're our newest $11 million winner.' The fine print, however, said the man was a winner only if he held the winning ticket. This was the second time in four months he had mistaken an entry for a winner and flown across the country to claim the prize.*"

Other letters to Ann Landers about sweepstakes also received big, bold, negative headlines, such as **"Sweepstakes Take Advantage With Their Wild, Personal Claims,"** and **"Niece Shocked by Aunt's Sweepstakes Addiction."** Ann Landers' replies were never favorable and generally pointed to the ongoing lawsuits. Again, columnists, consumers, and the media did not make a distinction between AFP and PCH. When they saw or read negative publicity about AFP or the sweepstakes industry, they just assumed the culprit was PCH.

The final example is the story of Dorothy Edouart, an elderly widow who was clearly addicted to playing sweepstakes. Her story received widespread news coverage, including an investigative report by *The New York Times*. Ms. Edouart spent about $60,000 over a five-year period on unread magazines and unused products from dozens of sweepstakes companies. When her children found out and objected to these expenses, she defiantly moved out of state to escape their objections. In heated disputes with her family, Ms. Edouart would tell them, "It's my money and I can do with it what I want." The sweepstakes obsession eventually drained her funds, and then she sued her son for the right to sell the family home. She needed money to keep playing sweepstakes and placing orders. The family sought to have her declared incompetent.

These are just three examples of the kind of negative media coverage and politics that PCH experienced for four long, painful years. I am not suggesting that some of this negative publicity was not deserved. PCH was not squeaky clean, and clearly there were consumers who had a problem. This included people like Richard Lusk and Dorothy Edouart, who beyond any doubt were addicted to entering sweepstakes. In most cases, however, even trusted family members couldn't stop their addiction and their buying.

I will be the first to admit that there were times when even the PCH Creative team went too far, and therefore we deserved the negative news coverage. An example of this was the front page article in the *Detroit News* in April 1997. In this front page story, Stephen Worhatch complained he had waited in vain for the PCH Prize Patrol in response to a PCH promotion asking him and his wife, bedridden with multiple sclerosis, to draw a map to their West Bloomfield home so the Prize Patrol could deliver a check for the first installment of a $10 million prize. Although a PCH executive pointed out that the fine print said the Prize Patrol "would come to your house if you were selected the winner," and there were other disclaimers in the promotion piece as well, many of us at PCH were not happy that we mailed this particular promotion.

In looking back at the entire situation, I am reluctant to disparage the press – but as I already said, the Arnold Diaz incident taught me that you can't believe what you hear or read in the news. So I will stick my neck out again and say that I take exception to the relentless and sometimes distorted stories from the news media in order to get better ratings. Out of countless negative stories about Publishers Clearing House, I never saw one single objective news report that indicated PCH was working hard to remedy the situation. I am not suggesting that the negative stories should not have been reported, just that there should have been some small semblance of balance.

All this negative publicity had a devastating effect on PCH and the entire direct marketing community. As stated, virtually overnight PCH's sales dropped 50%. In order to demonstrate how unprecedented the amount of negative news was for PCH, I offer the following comparisons with companies in two other industries that also went through extreme levels of negative publicity.

Toyota: In late 2009, the news started reporting a dangerous and potentially fatal sticking gas pedal problem for many Toyota models, ultimately leading to the largest ever recall in automotive history. Toyota eventually recalled more than eight million vehicles on five continents over a six-month period. Because this problem may have caused some deaths, Toyota, of course, received considerable negative publicity. The critical situation even prompted Congressional Hearings in early 2010. Toyota responsibly fixed the problem, but during the peak of their negative publicity in February 2010, Toyota's U.S. sales were reported to be down 9%.

British Petroleum (BP): The Deepwater Horizon oil spill on April 20, 2010, caused a disaster of unequaled proportion. The spill of roughly five million barrels of crude oil over about a four-month period resulted in an extreme amount of negative publicity directed at the oil giant. The news reported that BP-branded gas stations experienced sales declines of 10% to 40% during this period.

In comparison to Toyota's 9% sales decline and BP's 10% to 40% sales reduction, PCH's sales drop of 50% should demonstrate just how pervasive the negative publicity was for PCH. I should also note that the negative publicity for Toyota and British Petroleum lasted under six months, while PCH struggled through four years of negative news.

Now that I have described the situation with respect to the negative publicity directed at PCH and its impact on us, let me fully explain the situation with respect to the unrelenting lawsuits.

11

The Legal Troubles for PCH

It's Raining Lawsuits

When our legal problems started, we thought that our proactive measures with respect to addicted consumers, softening of our promotional language, earnest negotiations with the Attorneys General, considerate customer service policies, and past favorable relationships with the media would help us resolve the situation. We were, however, completely wrong about this.

By the late 1990's, fueled by all the adverse publicity, just about everyone was investigating, suing, and speaking disapprovingly about Publishers Clearing House. This included lawsuits from nearly every one of the fifty state Attorneys General, some suing individually and some banding together in joint lawsuits. Numerous individual private citizens were also suing PCH, as well as many lawyers across the country seeking class action status for lawsuits filed on behalf of thousands of consumers. Everyone was riding the bandwagon and taking advantage of the negative publicity. Even the big guns of the United States Senate were investigating, debating, and bad-mouthing sweepstakes at the Congressional Hearings.

At PCH, all we really wanted was to settle our legal woes, but it was impossible to get all the states' Attorneys General to agree with each other on a settlement. For example, a couple times, after months of long, intensive negotiations, we reached a tentative agreement with a handful of states, but then another group of states would balk at the potential settlement. A few other times, we reached an agreement with a group of assistant Attorneys General who were selected by their bosses to lead the negotiations, but when they took the settlement back to their superiors, the bosses would reject the settlement. As you can imagine, this made the situation impossibly difficult and frustrating.

To the dismay of our management team, the lawsuits and damaging news coverage continued for four years: starting with the Richard Lusk incident in late 1997, continuing past the Senate Hearings on sweepstakes in early 1999, continuing beyond our national class action settlement in mid-1999, continuing past the introduction of federal legislation in late 1999, and continuing even after PCH's settlement with twenty-four states in mid-2000. It was not until mid-year 2001 that the negative news coverage finally abated when PCH signed an agreement with the remaining group of twenty-six states.

Our lead lawyer and in-house legal counsel was Bill Low, a Senior Vice President with long tenure at PCH, and a Harvard Law graduate. Bill is as sharp and as dedicated as they come, and worked longer hours than anyone else I know. In addition, we received legal counsel from lawyers at our primary law firm, Morgan, Lewis, and Bockius, a prestigious international law firm located on New York's Park Avenue. Plus, we hired local legal counsel in the many states where we were being sued.

My colleague Bill Low summed it up best when he said to the press, "Prolonged litigation is very expensive, and no company can withstand separate proceedings with so many states." In fact, at this point our legal expenses had grown so high that the dozens of bright lawyers were costing us a fortune every year.

The basic charge of the lawsuits was deceptive advertising. Let me explain this allegation more fully so you can formulate your own opinion about the lawsuits we faced. Did you know, for example, that there are actually two definitions of "deceptive advertising," the dictionary definition and the legal definition? They differ only slightly, but in one very important way.

Dictionary definition: The dictionary defines "deceptive advertising" as advertising that makes false claims or misleading statements, as well as advertising that creates a false impression. Deceptive practices can take many forms such as false promises, unsubstantiated claims, incomplete descriptions, false testimonials or comparisons, small-print qualifications of advertisements, partial disclosure, or visual distortion of products.

Legal definition: According to advertising law, an advertisement is considered deceptive if it contains a statement or omits information that is likely to mislead consumers acting reasonably under the circumstances. To clarify, the law states that you have to tell the truth, so that no "**reasonable person**" could mistake your intent.

The key difference in the two definitions is marked in bold, referring to a "reasonable person."

My personal belief is that marketing and advertising from most companies in corporate America are to some degree deceptive according to the dictionary definition. Television commercials and print advertisements are always hyping a product's benefits or the like. The following are a few common sense examples of what is called "promotional hype." All are probably deceptive according to the "dictionary" definition, but not deceptive based on the "legal" definition.

1) Coors Light advertises itself as "the world's most refreshing beer." Is that claim really true? The average consumer clearly views this as a typical unsubstantiated advertising slogan.

2) The bus line my college-aged daughter regularly takes from Boston to New York and back, called the Bolt Bus, advertises that fares "start as low as $1.00 a seat." Although this may be technically true, most consumers know that very few seats really sell for that price. In the dozens of times my daughter has taken the bus, she has never gotten the $1.00 fare.

3) The New York State Lottery advertises that their "Take 5 – Little Bit of Luck" lottery has odds of winning at "1 in 9." Promoting these favorable odds in their massive television campaigns is clearly promotional hype, especially when consumers have to pay $1.00 to win a $1.00 prize or a "free play." I find it misleading to call someone a winner who pays $1.00 to win $1.00.

> Do you think the Attorneys General would let the sweepstakes mailers get away with promoting something like that? I think not.

With respect to PCH's promotions, management firmly believed that under the legal definition our promotions were not deceptive. In fact, in the dozen or so cases where a judge made a ruling on a PCH promotion, all judges expressed the same thing – that the PCH packages were not deceptive to a "reasonable person" and therefore legal. On the other hand, my personal belief is that AFP's promotion of the "Two Person Race" went too far and was deceptive, even under the legal definition.

With respect to Publishers Clearing House, I'll let you judge if we were remiss after giving both sides of the debate in the following pages. Regardless of what you decide, however, the real issue was that PCH could not get the states to agree with each other on a settlement, and that was the ongoing crux of our dilemma.

Senate Hearings

Senate Hearings on sweepstakes promotions took place on March 8 and 9, 1999. At the forefront of the debate was Senator Susan Collins from Maine, the Chairwoman of the Permanent Subcommittee on Investigations. Six other distinguished Senators were on this subcommittee and participated in the Hearings as well. This included Senator Carl Levin from Michigan, Senator Arlen Specter from Pennsylvania, Senator John Edwards from North Carolina, Senator Richard Durbin from Illinois, Senator Daniel Akaka from Hawaii, and Senator Ted Stevens from Alaska. In addition, the "Big Four" sweepstakes companies, as we were called, were "invited" via subpoena to attend and speak at the Hearings. These included Publishers Clearing House, Readers Digest, Time Inc., and American Family Publishers. Plus, there were two groups of witnesses. The first group was made up of victims of sweepstakes addiction and their families. The second group consisted of two expert witnesses, Virginia Tierney, a member of the Board of Directors at AARP, and Joseph Curran, Attorney General from Maryland.

Back at PCH, we knew the Senate Hearings were going to be brutal and expected heart-wrenching stories by victims and their families. I am not sure how we selected our representative to appear at the Hearings, but we sent our Senior Vice President in charge of Creative and Contest, Debbie Holland, to represent PCH. Debbie had been with PCH for twenty years and was known for her intelligence and loyalty in addition to being young, pretty, and petite. I'm nor sure why, but we didn't send our in-house Legal Counsel Bill Low, a Harvard Law graduate, to represent us. Nor did we send our Chairwoman, Robin Smith, a Harvard Business School graduate. I can only speculate that we hoped that perhaps the Senators would be more respectful and kind to Debbie, but boy, were we wrong. The Senators showed her absolutely no mercy.

Senator Collins opened the hearing by saying, "Let me emphasize that, to date, our investigation has uncovered no evidence that the sweepstakes offered by these particular companies are fraudulent. These companies run legitimate sweepstakes in the sense that all the prizes are awarded, none requires a purchase to enter the sweepstakes, and all entries are treated in equal fashion. Subsequently hearings will focus on promotional mailings that are outright fraudulent, such as the sweepstakes in which no prize is ever awarded. That is not the issue before us today." Senator Collins then went on to say, "We will examine how laws can be changed to make sweepstakes less deceptive and how the companies themselves could take steps to be more honest with the consumers receiving their mailings."

At this point, a few of the Senators delivered passionate opening statements, mostly speaking negatively about the sweepstakes mailers and recounting stories about their own constituents – like the one who "postponed needed surgery because she did not want to miss Ed McMahon's arrival with her winnings." After the Senators' opening statements, sweepstakes victims and family members recounted their troubling stories. Each story was more painful and upsetting than the next.

The first witness set the tone. A sobbing Eustace Hall became so emotional that his daughter had to finish his testimony. Mr. Hall, a retired sixty-five year old medical technologist, felt duped into spending $15,000 to $20,000 on sweepstakes purchases over the previous several years. He stated that he had to go back to work due to the debts he had incurred while playing sweepstakes. He admitted, "Playing the sweepstakes cost me a lot. I refinanced my house several times. And I had to borrow money from my pension fund four or five times to pay for my sweepstakes debts."

Another witness was Carol Gelinas, who told the moving story of her late father, Clyde Schott. When Ms. Gelinas took over her father's affairs, she was surprised to find that he had spent $60,000 on sweepstakes over the past fourteen years. Ms. Gelinas told the Senators, "I discovered that he was writing 30 to 40 checks each month, when his only bills were rent, telephone, and cable TV." She also stated that when she finally gained power of attorney, she found it very difficult to stop him. She testified, "Unfortunately, one outcome of these encounters was my father's suspicion that he really had won millions and that somehow I had taken it." Sadly for Ms. Gelinas, it had gotten to the point where her father was convinced that she had taken his prize money and used it to buy a new car and a vacation with her husband.

Another disturbing story was related by Dr. Stephanie Beukema, who described her mother's situation. Dr. Beukema conveyed about her mom, "She couldn't leave her home to visit family and friends overnight because she might miss a mailing or surprise visit from a company representative. She had to be there to get the mail every day." Dr. Beukema estimated that her mom had spent between $60,000 to $80,000 over an 18 to 24-month period. She also remarked that her mother's home was in danger of being repossessed for non-payment of taxes due to her mounting debts.

In yet another story, Dr. Karol Carter testified on behalf of her eighty-six year old father. Dr. Carter first indicated that her dad was upset with her for attending the Senate Hearings. She continued by saying, "He is concerned that I am ruining his chances of winning a Readers Digest sweepstakes when he, 'is getting close to winning.'" She told the Senators that her dad, who was retired from Chrysler Corporation, had a doctorate in organic chemistry. She then continued, "I have never questioned his intelligence, but since the sweepstakes began, all sense of reasoning with him has become impossible." Later on in her testimony she professed, "I cannot take control of the funds of a man who can still drive, shop, get to appointments, take medications properly, and care for my mother. He functions normally in every other way." In her opinion, her father was addicted to sweepstakes the way a person is addicted to liquor. Dr. Carter said, "If he were an alcoholic, he'd be dead drunk by now."

Other emotional stories of sweepstakes addicts were presented by their families as well, but I think I've reported enough on this front. Needless to say, each story was more disheartening than the next, and each revealed an unhealthy addiction to buying from dozens of sweepstakes companies. Most witnesses explained that their parents had mountains of products and magazine subscriptions filling their homes.

At one point in the Hearings, the matter of the odds of winning was discussed. On this subject, respected Senator Collins sarcastically expressed, "I was thinking that perhaps one way to inform consumers is if we required a very clear statement of odds using some information that was in the *Washington Post*, which is that your odds of dying from bites from venomous snakes, lizards, and spiders are greater than your odds of winning one of these major sweepstakes." The TV audience loved that remark.

Next up was Virginia Tierney, an AARP Board member. She quoted an AARP study that found that four out of ten respondents to their survey did not believe the statement, "*No purchase necessary to win*" with respect to sweepstakes mailings. Senator Akaka from Hawaii agreed with this sentiment when he stated, "I know from speaking with constituents that there is a strong and unwavering belief among too many Americans that a purchase is necessary to win."

Clearly, the small group of addicted consumers, like the ones in the aforementioned stories, took this mistaken belief to the extreme. The sad truth was apparent to everyone; even when implored by trusted family members to stop ordering (and that they didn't need to buy to win), some loved ones were too addicted to listen.

Finally, it was the Big Four's chance to present their cases, but first, Senator Richard Durbin from Illinois, missing from the prior day's session, made his opening statement. He noted that some had suggested that every sweepstakes mailing carry a warning label on the envelope. However, he acknowledged that the warning labels on cigarette packages haven't been very effective. Senator Durbin knew, as we all do, that warning labels don't really cure an addiction.

The Big Four representatives, including Debbie Holland, then presented their cases. In advance of the testimony, considerable background information and materials had already been submitted to the Senators (to help them prepare for the televised Hearings). A brief summary of Publishers Clearing House's oral and submitted testimony follows:

- Debbie Holland began by saying, "We recognize that there are some serious problems that must be addressed."

- Debbie also explained that PCH believed the problem was only with a very small percentage of customers. To prove this, she had submitted the following statistics on how much most customers spend with PCH in a typical year: "83 percent of the people who ordered anything from us in 1997 ordered less than $100 worth of magazines and products, and 95 percent ordered less than $300."

- To address the problem of "confused and addicted" customers, however, Debbie told the Senators, "While these individuals make up a very small fraction of a percent of our total customer population, Publishers Clearing House is very concerned about these individuals and feels an ethical responsibility to identify them and remove them from our mailing list."

- Debbie then reviewed how PCH had been very proactive the previous few years in trying to remedy the situation with the small number of overactive customers. As proof, the first victim who gave testimony at the Senate Hearings, Mr. Hall, had been identified and eliminated from all PCH mailings over a year before his testimony.

- The Senators knew that PCH had already implemented an internal system to identify and suppress from our mailings any customers who appeared to have an unhealthy amount of ordering. This was called the "High Activity Detection and Suppression" program and, in fact, I oversaw this program at the request of Robin Smith. We weren't perfect at it, but we tried, and although it definitely reduced our profits, we knew it was the ethical thing to do.

- My colleague further stated PCH's belief that the vast majority of Americans fully understood that no purchase was necessary. Debbie told the Senators, "The figures tell us, time and time again, that people know that winning big is a long shot and that they never have to buy anything to enter and win." Her testimony was supported by two hard facts. First: The data showed that 22 of 29, or 76%, of our big prize winners won on an entry that was not accompanied by an order. Second: Of those who did enter, there were always two, three, or even four times as many people who entered the sweepstakes without ordering as those who did. Both statistics indicate that the vast majority of consumers who entered our contest understood that they didn't have to buy anything to win.

- Debbie's testimony also described PCH's proactive customer service policies, which offered assistance to those who needed help with sweepstakes issues. First: "Publishers Clearing House maintains a special Sweepstakes Assistance Line at (800) 563-4724 available to family members or friends who may need help or assistance about a loved one who may be responding inappropriately to the promotions they are receiving." Second: "Customer service representatives are trained to spot customers who may need special assistance, and to handle inquiries in a humane and sympathetic manner backed by a liberal cancellation and refunds policy." Finally: When a problematic situation becomes known to us, either from a family member, friend, or other interested party, the customer's name will be removed from the PCH mailing list and a permanent block on orders will be placed on the customer's file.

- Debbie adamantly denied the additional accusation of targeting the elderly. She offered as proof the fact that our product offerings included items that appeal to all ages and all walks of life.

Debbie also stated that our market research indicated that most of our customers, about 70%, were under the age of sixty-five.

- The Senators were also reminded that Publishers Clearing House mailings had been tested in the courts many times over the past few years, and in each instance were found to be lawful. In one typical example, Magistrate Judge Cogburn in the United States District Court for the Western District of North Carolina, in dismissal of a case against PCH, stated, "a reasonable person could not have concluded that he had won $10 million based upon the mailings annexed to plaintiff's complaint." Other similar rulings in favor of PCH were also recounted, including the District of Oregon and the Eastern District of Kentucky. In addition, it was pointed out that, "In no case has a Publishers Clearing House mailing been found to be deceptive or misleading, or otherwise to have violated any law."

Sadly, none of the information presented at the Senate Hearings really seemed to matter to the Senators. The Senators didn't even appear to be listening, and it was disheartening that PCH received absolutely no credit for our proactive measures. It is my belief that the other sweepstakes mailers were not as proactive, if at all, and that played against PCH. For example, at the Hearings one victim said, "Two of the biggest problems I had were with Readers Digest and Time-Life audio tapes."

It seemed that the Senators' sole purpose was to show the news media and the public how compassionate they could be to the victims and their families while at the same time to get the Big Four to admit they were wrong. The Senators' questions and accusations were relentless, and they attacked Debbie Holland mercilessly.

Senator Collins singled Debbie out by telling her she was "absolutely stunned" by her testimony that no "reasonable person" could be misled by PCH's mailings. Other Senators, equally unkind, used words like "appalled," "deeply distressed," and "perfectly a lie" with respect to Debbie's testimony. It was like a feeding frenzy with a school of hungry sharks surrounding a brave, lone goldfish.

After watching the live televised Hearings and reading the transcripts afterwards, I agree with what the press often reports about Senate

Hearings – that they are often just a political sideshow.

Addiction to anything, be it alcohol, cigarettes, gambling, or sweepstakes, is certainly dreadful. But are addicts "reasonable?" This was the real issue, and it wasn't really addressed. I know someone who lost his job, his home, and his entire family due to gambling. It was very tragic. I also know someone who was addicted to drinking Coke. He drank nearly a dozen cans of Coke at work each day. I'm not sure if he is still alive. Can we say these two people are reasonable? One lost his family, and the other possibly shortened his life. Neither demonstrated reasonable behavior, but sadly, neither behavior is illegal according to the law.

At one point during the Hearings, Senator Durbin made what I thought was an interesting and insightful comment. He lectured: "We live in a nation and in a society where government condones lotteries which prey on poor and elderly people. We live in a society where government condones and licenses gaming and casinos, where we know that the poor and the elderly show up and spend a lot of money that they should not spend, and I cannot make any excuse for either of those." Based on his statement, you would think that the Senators would be attacking casinos and their very own state lotteries the same way they were attacking sweepstakes. But, of course, they weren't.

About nine months after the Senate Hearings concluded, on December 12, 1999, federal legislation regarding sweepstakes was passed into law. The major aspects of the new law, called the "Deceptive Mail Prevention and Enforcement Act," required direct mail sweepstakes promotions to include the following provisions in their mailings:

- The official rules must disclose the odds of winning.

- A statement that "No purchase is necessary" must appear three times in all promotional mailings, and this language must be conspicuous to the consumer.

- A statement that a purchase doesn't improve an individual's chances of winning must also appear three times in all promotional mailings, and must also be conspicuous to the consumer.

I believe the legislation that passed was fair and appropriate, although I don't think any of it will really deter an addicted consumer. The Senate Hearings, however, in my opinion, were a complete waste of time. If the Senators spent less time posturing and politicking, and more time doing, everyone would be much better off.

In spite of the new federal legislation, this did not stop the onslaught of lawsuits against PCH and the rest of the sweepstakes industry.

National Class Action Settlement

All this time, PCH had been trying to settle our legal issues through many channels. It was shortly after the Senate Hearings took place that we thought we had finally reached a settlement that resolved all our legal woes.

After considerable negotiation, on June 30, 1999, U.S. District Judge G. Patrick Murphy approved a settlement in a national class action lawsuit filed on behalf of all consumers who received PCH solicitations. As part of the agreement, PCH agreed to offer $30 million in refunds in a mailing to our entire customer file.

Our class action mailing to 43 million PCH customers was the largest single mailing to a class action group in U.S. history. Just to implement this large a mailing cost well over $10 million in printing and postage, in addition to the $30 million in refunds. This was the first class action settlement by a sweepstakes company (and another important project that I was asked to oversee). Similar class action lawsuits were pending against AFP, Time Inc., Readers Digest, and others.

At PCH we were absolutely thrilled to have a settlement. We believed this would finally put all our legal problems behind us, although we were not happy with the $30 million plus price tag. However, to our complete and utter astonishment, and to the surprise of our numerous advisors, the national class action settlement only made matters worse.

The class action settlement apparently made dozens of Attorneys General irate. We were never told why, but we speculated it was because the states themselves didn't get any money out of the settlement. It also probably didn't help that the politicians would lose all that powerful publicity from going after the "evil PCH." We could not believe that the class action settlement itself was vehemently opposed by most of the states, and this caused yet another flurry of negative publicity and additional lawsuits.

One example was Colorado Attorney General Ken Salazar's announcement that he was joining twenty other state Attorneys General in filing formal comments objecting to the class action settlement. The headline of his press release read, "**COLORADO ATTORNEY GENERAL OBJECTS TO NATIONAL CLASS ACTION SETTLEMENT WITH PUBLISHERS CLEARING HOUSE.**" Mr. Salazar didn't like the wording of the settlement mailing, which he thought was too confusing. In actuality, we had drafted a very simple settlement notice, but it was rejected by the court, so the notice was rewritten by the opposing class action lawyers.

In similar fashion, a headline in Iowa read, "**Miller Questions Publishers Clearing House Class Action Settlement.**" This was from Attorney General Tom Miller, who said, "We have serious questions about this settlement." He went on to claim, "We are particularly concerned that PCH may target older citizens with frequent personalized mailings that tend to deceive them."

And in yet another example were charges from Attorney General Bob Butterworth of Florida, whose press release included this headline: "**Butterworth Urges Floridians To Consider Opting Out of Publishers Clearing House Settlement; Readies Own Complaint Against Company.**"

These are just a few examples of the negative reactions by the Attorneys General to our national class action settlement. So here we were back at square one, with dozens of impending lawsuits, continued negative publicity, and no end in sight.

Attorneys General Lawsuits

By the end of 1999, the Senate Hearings were over, the new federal legislation on sweepstakes had passed, and we had completed a large settlement in a national class action lawsuit. But the litigation against us continued.

At this point, the vast majority of the fifty states were waging a full-scale war against PCH, which to our dismay was battled conspicuously in the press.

In January 2000, a new seventeen state lawsuit was filed against PCH. What made the whole situation worse was that this kind of action meant not one, but numerous press releases. Each Attorney General wanted to show that each was out to protect the consumers in his or her own state. For example, California's Bill Lockyer's press release read, "**Publishers Clearing House for years has been targeting the elderly and the gullible with a blizzard of deceptive mailers that are really disguised sales pitches.**" Just about every state Attorney General had a similar negative press release.

As mentioned earlier, the dilemma was that we couldn't get the states to agree with each other. And each state wanted something different from PCH. Internally, we talked about the fact that we could likely win every individual lawsuit, but the cost to fight them all would put us out of business.

It didn't help the negotiations that the types of things for which some Attorneys General were asking were outlandish. Some had a list of demands that went on for dozens of pages. Some wanted all PCH customers who had spent more than a few hundred dollars a year with us, not just confused customers, to be refunded all the money they had spent plus eliminated from all future mailings. Could any business survive by refunding all the money their best customers spent and eliminating them from future business?

In other cases, some of the states were seeking unreasonable amounts of money from us. For example, Florida's Attorney General Bob Butterworth was seeking $40 million for just his state alone. To put this in perspective, if we settled with all the suing states for half that amount, it would have cost PCH $1 billion. Even a small fraction of that amount would have forced us to just shut our doors.

So after more depressing publicity and little progress on the legal front, we decided to try a completely different approach. We thought that perhaps we should hire a very high-powered, politically connected force to help with our legal activities, especially with our negotiations with the numerous Attorneys General.

We considered several influential individuals for the assignment. The most well-known and highly regarded was none other than George

Mitchell (previous Senator for fifteen years, Special Advisor to President Clinton, receiver of the Presidential Medal of Freedom, and subsequently named Special Envoy for Middle East Peace under President Obama). In fact, Mr. Mitchell traveled to PCH one day to discuss working with us. Unexpectedly tall and stylishly dressed in an expensive black business suit, he was an impressive looking visitor. In the end, however, PCH selected Ben Civiletti, a former United States Attorney General to help us out.

Almost three years after the initial American Family Publishers incident, in August 2000, PCH finally completed a settlement with about half of the states (twenty-four to be exact). This settlement included $18 million in restitution.

Many states, however, were still not satisfied. For example, speaking negatively about the new twenty-four state settlement, a spokesman for Attorney General Mark Pryor of Arkansas asserted, "The settlement didn't go far enough." He wanted PCH to make more changes to our marketing practices and provide additional refunds to consumers.

It was not until almost another year later, at long last, in June 2001, that PCH settled all remaining allegations with the remaining twenty-six states. In this final settlement, we paid another $34 million.

It took four long, destructive years, but the PCH legal ordeal was finally over, and we could get back to business. Back at PCH we were thrilled, but it had certainly taken its toll on us – financially, emotionally, and personally.

12   The Roller Coaster Ride Down

The Bad Times at PCH

As reported previously, after almost fifty years of monumental growth, suddenly in early 1999 the bottom dropped out. Not only were we battling seemingly never-ending lawsuits, but we were also struggling to survive.

PCH profits dropped from a huge gain the previous year to a large loss… something we were totally unprepared for. The irony was that we had just completed several years of massive hiring and restructuring and had put in place a staff of over 1,000 full-time employees, essentially doubling the size of our full-time staff. We were finally able to handle and manage $1 billion in annual sales when the roller coaster took its sharp plunge down.

An article on the sweepstakes giants in *Advertising Age*, a trade publication, reported what the magazine industry already knew: "Publishers are estimating the subscription orders are down by as much as 30% to 50%." At the time, we tried to put on our best face and told publishers and the press that our results were off, but not as much as the news reported.

The truth was that PCH's sales dropped like a rock. Our sales plummeted about 40% in one year's time and by about 60% over a two-year period. Our profits dropped even more, to our first ever loss. With our large new infrastructure in place, we now had some severe cost cutting to do. At the moment, fortunately, we had plenty of cash reserves and no debt, so we weren't too worried.

For the first time ever, PCH had to lay people off. The initial round of layoffs took place in November 1999, affecting about 20% to 25% of our workforce, or 213 employees. This wasn't easy for us, especially due to the large number of employees involved. We began our downsizing by offering early retirement to many workers, with very generous severance packages; this made it far less painful.

Over the next few years, though, our losses continued to mount with no end in sight, so we had to have phases two, three, four and five of layoffs and cost-cutting initiatives. Each successive round got harder and harder, and needless to say, our severance packages became less and less generous. By the fourth or fifth round of layoffs, we had no choice but to let go many dedicated, hard-working, loyal employees, some of whom had been part of the PCH family for many years.

The employees who were let go in the early stages fared well. However, in the later rounds, severance was cut to an absolute minimum, as we just couldn't afford it anymore. The employees who left displayed many different emotions, including sorrow, disappointment, anger, and rage, but the most common reaction was tears. In total, over 50% of our PCH family was eventually terminated.

We also reduced overhead in all areas, and this was done in many phases as well. We called the first round "the low hanging fruit." But later rounds, of course, got more and more challenging. All totaled, we eliminated hundreds of millions of dollars in overhead and mailing costs. As we squeezed our long-time suppliers more and more, some eventually couldn't handle the fee cuts and went out of business.

The severe cost-cutting was painful but imperative if we were to survive. Sadly, even after a few years of deep cuts, it was still not enough, and we continued to lose money. In addition, we had been spending millions of dollars for our legal settlements, totaling over $80 million in the end. By 2001 our cash reserves were virtually gone, and the senior management team, myself included, was very, very worried.

At this point, we were having severe cash flow problems. To add insult to injury, at the worst possible time, our longstanding, trusted banking partner EAB called in our line of credit. We were forced to immediately pay back $37 million, so we quickly sought financing elsewhere, but were turned down due to the plethora of lawsuits. The many loan rejections added to our anxiety and concern. As a last resort, we were able to attain some much needed financing, $29 million, in July 2002, from CIT Business Credit (a unit of CIT Group Inc.). The terms of the loan, however, were onerous. If we didn't make our hefty interest payments on time, they would close us down and take the buildings, the furniture, the land, and the receivables.

Around this time, another challenge presented itself. This problem came from our large supplier base. Our reputation had been that we always paid our bills on time, but this was no longer the case. We had no choice but to start deferring payment of our larger bills, and, in turn, some of our suppliers started to get worried. Several had already been burnt by bankruptcies in our industry, so it wasn't really surprising that they were worried about PCH.

I was a Senior Vice President during this challenging period, responsible for most of the cost centers at PCH. The situation got so bad that I started to receive anxious phone calls from many of our suppliers who were wondering why their bills weren't being paid. I would tell the callers that there was nothing to worry about, but that I would check with the Finance department about their invoices. I would then call our Finance department, who informed me what I already knew – that they were holding some of our larger bills for a few months, but that these invoices would be paid. In my calls back to the suppliers, I had no choice but to say that the invoices were just held up in all the paperwork that our Finance department receives and that they would be paid shortly.

For one of our larger suppliers, this answer wasn't good enough. RR Donnelley, one of our many printers, wanted to have a face-to-face meeting with me and our VP of Finance, John McCusker, to discuss our late payments. We reluctantly arranged a meeting, and the President of the RR Donnelley print division and their Finance VP came out to PCH. At this difficult meeting they demanded that we pay all our outstanding bills immediately and also guarantee that future bills be paid within thirty days of receipt, or they would not accept any more work from us.

We had anticipated this and had already planned our response. We called their bluff and played hardball. We knew we couldn't show any signs of weakness. John McCusker assured them by stating, "Our finances are fine, and we will continue to process your bills through our normal channels." Then I chimed in, "If that isn't acceptable, there are plenty of other printers out there who would love to get our business. It's up to you."

We weren't sure how they would react, but RR Donnelley blinked first. They remained a supplier and never questioned our delayed payments again. It's a good thing they didn't know the extent of our cash flow problem. If they had known and it had spread to other suppliers, that would have made a bad problem worse – perhaps even the proverbial straw that broke the camel's back. This was the only situation where I ever lied to our suppliers, co-workers, or staff members… but I really had no choice.

The publicity about PCH and sweepstakes was so pervasive and so negative, and our results were so brutally low, that at one point we even considered whether to abandon sweepstakes altogether.

So at the height of the negative publicity, we decided to test a promotion without sweepstakes. When the results came in, they surprised us all. Despite the widespread negative press, the test results indicated that we did better with sweeps than without. We speculated that this was probably because our name was just so synonymous with sweepstakes. Perhaps if we had had more time, we could have made the change. But time was running out, so this was not an option.

With our losses mounting, as well as our legal fees and settlement costs, and still no end in sight, we considered the possibility of reorganization under the protection of bankruptcy. We thought that if we filed Chapter 11, it could wipe out all the lawsuits… and we could potentially start over. Our major competitor, AFP, had filed for voluntary Chapter 11 bankruptcy in late 1999. They hoped it would help resolve their lawsuits and enable them to restructure their finances and operations in order to survive. About a year later, however, they closed their doors permanently.

Our new VP of Finance, John McCusker, was hired in part because he had experience in bankruptcy. The top brass also met with outside legal counsel that specialized in this action. The legal advice, however, raised a potential major problem with this approach. The PCH partners themselves could be asked to pony up cash in bankruptcy; this made the discussion moot as this was not an option.

PCH also considered asking for a large infusion of cash as a loan from the only partner who could possibly help. That was Esther Mertz, Harold Mertz's second wife, but she would have wanted control of the company in return. Robin Smith, Chairman and CEO, was opposed to this.

Around this time, at one of our monthly Executive meetings with all the Vice Presidents, Robin Smith declared that we needed to have yet another round of cost cutting in all corners of the company. This was something like the sixth round, and as I said, each time was more difficult than the last. At this somber meeting, Robin asked for a volunteer to lead this company-wide effort. There were about ten of us in the conference room, and there was complete and utter silence. Robin turned her head in my direction, her look urging me to volunteer for the assignment. I knew there was a clear choice – either more cost-cutting and more layoffs or something far worse.

I led this company-wide effort, working closely with each of the Vice Presidents to identify more cuts and more staff reductions. My perspective was that we could either cut as deep as possible or we could all just go home – meaning bankruptcy. I would use these exact words at many of the meetings where we belabored and battled over additional cost-cutting measures.

I submitted my report to Robin with the additional company-wide cuts. We came up with another $30 to $40 million in annual cost savings, which may seem modest, but these additional cuts were like getting blood from a stone since they were on top of the enormous cuts we had already implemented over the past few years. All of the recommended cost cuts were quickly implemented.

The Golden Egg

In addition to the cost cuts, we were desperately looking for some way to boost sales. Around this time, one of our young rising stars in the Marketing department came up with a new profit-making idea which would make a ton of money right away. His proposal was to start a new program called the "Continuity" program, which would sell collectible-type items like coins, dolls, figurines, and the like, in a continuous series to our existing customers. Consumers would only order once, and shipments would automatically be sent on a monthly or regular basis. This is the business model that companies like the Bradford Exchange and Danbury Mint were operating under.

This young Marketing Manager submitted the proposal to his boss, Senior Vice President of Marketing, Andy Goldberg. The new program was projected to make a tidy amount at $50 million profit in the very first year. The great news went directly to Robin Smith, our CEO, who quickly informed the PCH Executive Committee (our partners and owners) of the much needed good news.

A few weeks later, the President, Bruce Pantano, came to see me and asked if I would look at the detailed plan for the new program. I reported to Bruce for many years, and we respected and trusted each other and treated one another as confidants. Bruce was skeptical about the Continuity plan and wanted me to fully evaluate and check the numbers.

I should point out that the entire philosophy of the company had recently changed. The old approach of evaluating and reporting on everything was gone, as was the style to openly debate important issues. This change in style was due to the massive downsizing (not having enough staff to run the business) and the less open personal style of the soon to be new President. In the old days, the detailed plan for a new program like this would have been passed around to all the Vice Presidents, and a full debate would have occurred. But this was a new world, and a new style, and the detailed plan had not been given to the rest of the senior management team, including me.

I, of course, agreed to look at the plan, and upon receiving it, I took it home that very evening. I was hoping that the profit projection was correct or at least close to being correct. However, with my long marketing background, I spotted two major flaws. This would not be good news, and I was disheartened by my conclusion. Unfortunately, my corrections would change the profit projection from $50 million per year to close to ZERO.

In layman's terms, here is what I found:

The first major flaw concerned the issue of "free credit." At PCH, all programs used this promotional tool, which meant we would mail the customer a bill for the purchase price of the item ordered. We never asked for cash up front, and we didn't accept credit card payments. Because of this "soft offer," as it was called, about 10% to 20% of buyers normally ended up not paying us, either because they were cancelling their subscription or returning an item, or because they were just ripping us off. The new Continuity program used the typical PCH "free credit" offer, and that was fine. However, the plan assumed that 2% to 3% of buyers wouldn't pay. This assumption should have been around 10% to 20%, which was the norm for a PCH mailing.

The second major flaw dealt with what we called "stolen revenue." The new Continuity program assumed that the added sales would be 100% incremental to all other programs at PCH. Based on lots of prior testing, however, we knew that whenever we introduced a new program to our customer base, the sales from the new program were only about 75% to 80% incremental. That meant that when we added mailings to the same customers, it would lower, or steal, sales from the mailings immediately before and after the newly added effort. This adjusted for the fact that customers would only buy so much at a time. The stolen revenue factor for the Continuity program should have been about 20%, but instead 0% was assumed.

I regrettably took this information to Bruce Pantano, who fully agreed with my assessment and distressing conclusion. Bruce had no choice but to take my analysis to Robin, and I was relieved that he chose to tell her the bad news in a one-on-one private meeting.

I don't know how Robin reacted to the news, but I am sure she wasn't happy. I also don't know if Robin believed my conclusions or if she informed the Executive Committee of my findings. What I do know is that she never said a word to me about my assessment, and we proceeded with the new program full speed ahead.

The new program took a lot of company time, energy, and resources at a time when we had been downsizing, but in typical PCH style, we got the job done. It was not very long before actual results showed that the Continuity program would not be the money-maker it was originally presented to be, so it was soon scaled back dramatically. I'm not sure if the Continuity program still exists today or not. What I do know is that the young marketing superstar who initiated the program is gone.

2001

Although our legal issues had been resolved in mid-year 2001, the cost cuts weren't doing the trick and the Golden Egg was a dud. So at this point, we were still limping along financially and needed to get back in the black, or we wouldn't survive. We forged ahead and focused our energies on rebuilding the business that Harold Mertz had started and built. But it wasn't going to be easy.

13 The Penalty Doesn't Fit the Crime

|||||||||||||||||||||||||||||||||||||||||||||||||||||||||||||||||||||||||||||||||||||||||||||||||||||||||||||||||||||||||||||||||||||||

Not many companies or industries could survive four years of damaging negative publicity and countless lawsuits. For the sweepstakes and direct marketing communities, the outcome was complete financial devastation. There would, in fact, be very few survivors.

By the end of 2001, all the multi-magazine subscription agents went belly-up except Publishers Clearing House. This included American Family Publishers, who shut their doors in April 2001, in spite of its two very wealthy owners. All the smaller multi-magazine agencies went under as well including Magazine Marketplace, Great American Magazines, and others. Employees at all these companies were terminated. At American Family Publishers, surprisingly, none of the displaced workers were offered jobs at the parent company, Time Inc.

It turned out that Publishers Clearing House would be the sole surviving multi-magazine agency. But its business became a shell of its former self, and the PCH staff was cut by 50% or over 500 full-time workers.

Many other companies that used sweepstakes also went out of business. Two of the largest were Foster and Gallagher, a popular gardening supply cataloger, and U.S. Purchasing Exchange, a major direct marketer of low-ticket merchandise. Many more workers at these companies lost their jobs as well.

The magazine industry was hit especially hard. Approximately 300 magazines were forced to cut their rate base (the number of readers guaranteed to advertisers) because the number of new subscribers generated by the sweepstakes promotions dropped to almost nothing – from about 50 million subscriptions per year to only a few million a year. Because of this, the staffs at virtually every publisher in the United States had to be dramatically reduced. This included massive layoffs at two of the largest publishers in the world, Readers Digest Association and Time Inc. The staff at Readers Digest, for example, dropped by 80%, from 4,000 to 800. Publishing industry expert Jack Brittan summed up the situation by declaring, "A critical tool in circulation building died when the sweeps companies were battered."

In addition, hundreds of suppliers around the country felt the aftershocks and were negatively impacted, and some even went out of business. This resulted in more employees out of work. The list of displaced workers came from lettershops, printers, paper manufacturers, fulfillment houses, and more.

The impact of the collapse of the sweepstakes industry would, in fact, be felt for many years. Almost ten years later, the esteemed Readers Digest Association still couldn't climb out of its downward spiral. The result was that in August 2009 the parent company of the most widely read magazine in the world, with over 100 million readers in sixty countries and in twenty-one languages, filed for Chapter 11 bankruptcy protection. Readers Digest has since reorganized and is a much different and smaller business today.

In addition to all of this devastation, another major supplier of the direct marketing community, one that is rarely mentioned, was also crippled by the destruction of the sweepstakes community. That supplier was the United States Postal Service, who was out a huge amount of money – billions of dollars, in fact. The four biggest sweepstakes mailers alone, PCH, AFP, Readers Digest, and Time Inc., were mailing close to 1.5 billion pieces of promotional mail per year while generating millions of magazine subscriptions and selling a large number of low-ticket merchandise as well. The postage paid to the USPS every year by direct marketers had been enormous. The loss in postal revenue included promotional mail, monthly or weekly magazine subscriptions, product parcels, billing notices, and renewal notices. Over the nine years since

I retired from PCH, I estimate the postal service is out about $6 to $7 billion in postage due to the total collapse of the sweepstakes industry. That may be why the financial situation of the USPS is so dire today. The USPS is projecting a net loss of billions of dollars for 2011.

Another by-product of the devastation were charities and nonprofit organizations. Since over 40% of PCH profits went to charitable causes and the like, these programs suffered immensely. All counted, these organizations had been receiving an average of about $50 million a year from the Mertz family trusts and foundations in each of the previous ten years that PCH was profitable. But with PCH in the red, they received "nada," which was the case for the last four years I worked at PCH. There was absolutely no credit or even acknowledgement of the Mertz family's charitable giving from the Attorneys General nor the politicians. A similar scenario was true for the significant philanthropic activities by Readers Digest.

When all summed up, the bottom line from the destruction of the sweepstakes industry was that tens of thousands of employees lost their jobs, and the impact was felt throughout the direct marketing community, the numerous suppliers who supported the industry, the United States Postal Service, and charitable organizations.

In reflecting back on the entire situation, I agree that some of the sweepstakes promotions went too far, especially the infamous AFP promotion. I also concur that we all needed to soften our promotional language to some degree (and the federal legislation took care of that). In addition, there is no denying that there were individuals who were sadly addicted to sweepstakes, similar to those addicted to alcohol or gambling. And I believe, of course, that we should do everything in our power to help these individuals.

In the case of sweepstakes addiction, an easy compromise could have been for PCH, as well as all the other sweepstakes companies, to determine a process whereby addicted or confused consumers were eliminated from all sweepstakes mailings. This was, in fact, what PCH had been doing for the few years prior to the passage of federal legislation. Unfortunately, even though we were able to stop most addicted and confused consumers from buying from us, our proactive measures didn't matter in the least to the politicians and the Attorneys General.

I also believe the zeal with which virtually all of the states' Attorneys General went after PCH was totally unconscionable. And the fact that the states could not agree with each other on a settlement with PCH was simply outrageous. They really didn't have to destroy an entire industry. I have never seen Attorneys General attacking and closing down state run lotteries, casinos or liquor stores. These industries have the same problem of addiction. And it is common knowledge that casinos pull in those less fortunate, and no secret that the most frequent buyers of the Attorneys General's very own state lotteries are the poor. *Why weren't the Attorneys General concerned with the poor consumers addicted to liquor, gambling, and lottery-buying in their very own states?*

Finally, I find it objectionable and disingenuous that many of the highly publicized statements by the numerous Attorneys General and politicians were simply using PCH's well-known name to their own advantage. These powerful individuals seemed more interested in publicity than in actually resolving the problem.

I remember asking my esteemed colleague Bill Low, Senior VP and General Counsel at PCH, on one of the many frustrating days dealing with the whole legal quagmire, "Why are they attacking us? We're the good guys."

His answer was, "Because we are an easy target with a big name. The bad guys, the scam artists and companies that don't award their prizes are not as easy a target because they will change their name, change their location, and carry on."

14 The Worst Three Hours of My Life

As difficult, depressing, and debilitating as the previous four years at PCH had been for me, dealing with the legal mess, the negative publicity, layoffs, and cost cuts, it pales in comparison to these three hours of my life.

This will undoubtedly be the most difficult chapter for me to write. It's about that shocking, disturbing, and devastating day... September 11, 2001. It's been ten years, and I still haven't watched any of the press recaps, movies, or documentaries about that day. I can't, and I won't watch them – it's just too emotionally difficult. I am tearing up just writing this story. I am including this chapter to share with you the story of my five-minute older identical twin brother that awful day, while I sat in my comfortable teak-lined office, and the tremendous kindness that afternoon from the leader of PCH.

It started like any other typical busy day. I arrived at work early and was working at my desk when I heard a commotion outside my office. I heard rumblings that a small plane had hit one of the World Trade Center's Twin Towers. It was slightly before 9:00 a.m. (the first plane hit at 8:46). We had several television sets at PCH headquarters, and they were all immediately switched on. One TV was right outside my office.

My brother, Dennis, worked at the World Trade Center in one of the two Towers. I had no idea what floor he was on or which Tower he worked in. At this point, I wasn't really worried. The initial news reports continued to say that it appeared that a small plane had hit the Tower. But then at 9:03 a.m., the second Tower was hit. The only thing

I knew for sure at this moment was that my brother was in one of the two Towers. I knew this because Dennis never called in sick and always arrived at work early. I immediately tried to contact him at both his office number and on his cell phone, many times, but no one answered. It was disconcerting that he didn't answer his cell phone since I knew he had it with him. Dennis always wore his cell phone strapped to his belt; my family and I used to joke that he slept and showered wearing his cell phone.

Nobody did any work that day. We all watched the television news in shock and horror. The more I watched, the worse it got. I still couldn't get in touch with my brother. I called family members, but nobody knew what floor he was on, and no one had heard from him.

Then the absolute unthinkable happened. At 9:59 a.m., the South Tower imploded and in a moment's time disintegrated into a cloud of debris. And then at 10:28 a.m., the North Tower collapsed. The scenes on television were utterly devastating. I have never felt so angry and helpless in my entire life. The more I watched on TV, the more horrific it got. I can't really describe my anger, rage, and fear, except to say – for the first time in my life – I felt I could kill someone with my bare hands.

I couldn't sit, so I paced up and down, watching the news. I kept trying to reach Dennis on his cell phone. Never an answer… and I knew he had his cell phone with him. At this point, as you can imagine, I was agonizing beyond belief. After every unanswered phone call, I sank deeper and deeper into despair.

Finally, at exactly noon, on about my hundredth call to Dennis, he answered his cell phone. I was the first one to have reached him and was shocked when he picked up. Astonished and surprised, I simply said, "Dennis?"

I remember his exact words. He said back to me, "I'm OK, I'm OK, just trying to get out of the city. I will call you back as soon as I can. Tell everyone I am OK." And then click, he hung up. I went to my office, sat down, and the tears poured out, tears of unbelievable joy and relief! He was safe!

Of course, it got around PCH headquarters pretty fast that my brother was okay. Shortly after, I happened to be walking past Robin Smith's office, and she called me in. She knew that it would be nearly impossible for Dennis to get out of the city because all transportation in and out of the city had been stopped. Robin kindly offered her Manhattan apartment for him to stay in that night. She told me she could leave a message with the doorman who would let him in. I very much appreciated the thoughtful and compassionate offer, and told her I would talk to Dennis and let her know.

Now let me tell you the story of that day as it was told to me by my brother and my very best friend.

Dennis was on the 24th floor of the first Tower hit. He was sitting at his desk, early as usual, around 8:00 a.m. It started just like any other day for him as well, when a member of his staff came in to discuss a business issue. They were in his office, which had a breathtaking view of the Manhattan skyline, having a heated debate about a business problem. About ten minutes into their argument they heard a loud noise, and they both felt the building physically move. Dennis has said that he is not sure how much the building really moved, but it felt like it moved at least a foot. They also noticed dust flying around inside, as if someone were shaking out an old dirty blanket. Outside his window they could see falling debris. There were no alarms, no announcements of any kind, and the lights and power remained on.

After a few minutes of bewilderment, Dennis and everyone else on the floor slowly started walking towards the exit stairs to head down the twenty-four flights to exit the building. There was no panic. No one knew what had happened, but everyone instinctively felt they should get out of the building.

It took a very long time to walk down the twenty-four flights of stairs. Everyone seemed to be leaving the building at the same time, and firemen in full gear were on their way up. This slowed their exit as everyone made room for the firemen. Dennis says he can still see the faces of the brave men going up the stairs, very young, healthy, physically fit men in full fire gear. When Dennis finally got to the second floor there were about two inches of water covering the floor. People were stopping to take off their shoes, but Dennis just rolled up his pants. At this point, no one in the stairwells had any idea as to what had happened.

It wasn't until Dennis entered the lower lobby, after thirty-five minutes of walking down the stairs, that he realized that something terrible had happened. The enormous and beautiful lobby of the World Trade Center was completely disintegrated and in total ruin. Apparently, the blast from the crash and fire on the top floors blew down the elevator shafts and out the lobby, completely obliterating everything in its path. If you had ever seen the lobby of the Twin Towers, it was a luxurious expanse with dozens of stores, shops, and restaurants. As Dennis walked into the lobby, it was gone, completely and utterly gone! Broken glass, cement and debris were everywhere. It looked to Dennis like a bomb had exploded in the lobby.

Dennis finally stepped outside, and there was a police officer directing everyone exiting the building. The cop kept repeating loudly, "Walk south, and do not look back or up." Of course, the first thing Dennis did was to look back and up. My brother was never any good at following directions. As he looked up, he saw immense flames and billowing smoke at the top of both Twin Towers. Dennis says this image is permanently etched in his mind. He says it felt like he was watching a movie… and that it all felt so surreal. He would have no part of walking south, though, as directed by the cop. He instinctively headed north towards Pennsylvania Station, which would at least be in the direction of home.

It turned out that Dennis's decision not to listen to the police officer was a good one. His boss and about ten of his colleagues followed the cop's directions and went south. They were only able to get a dozen or so blocks since the World Trade Center was close to the southern tip of Manhattan, which we all know is an island surrounded by water. When the Towers collapsed a huge plume of dirty black dust, debris, and smoke descended upon his colleagues. Dennis's boss told him afterwards that as the group he was with saw the wall of smoke coming at them, they all just lay down on the ground and prayed, with no idea what was going to happen. They luckily survived, but covered in dust and debris.

Dennis said that on his way to Pennsylvania Station, his cell phone rang over and over again. That was me calling him. But when he tried to answer the calls, there was no one on the other end. From what I have been told, the calls couldn't get through because there were so many cell phone calls being made. All along the way there were pay phones, but long lines of people were waiting to use them. Dennis wanted to call home, but he didn't want to wait on the lines, so he just kept walking.

When he got to Pennsylvania Station, there were thousands of people mulling around in the street. So Dennis, in a daze from the chaos, walked down the stairs into Penn Station. When he got near the Long Island Railroad entrance, he stopped and noticed that he was there all by himself. It was a ghost town. There would normally be scores of hustling and bustling people where he was standing, but there was not a living soul in sight. At that moment, a cop approached him and yelled, "You know Penn Station is closed and no trains are running. You aren't supposed to be down here!" Dennis simply replied, "Oops," and walked back out towards the thousands of people in the street.

At this point, Dennis had heard people saying that the Twin Towers had collapsed. He had seen the Towers on fire, but he did not believe the rumors that the Towers had actually fallen.

After about ten minutes of wandering around with everyone else, Dennis ran into two friends from work. They talked about what to do and decided, for lack of anything else to do, to walk toward the Midtown Tunnel. At least this was in the direction of getting out of the city and going home. I am not sure what they were thinking because you can't walk through the Midtown Tunnel.

They saw some fighter jets overhead, and people in the streets were cowering on the ground fearful of some kind of attack, but Dennis and his two buddies just kept walking. They got about a block from the Midtown Tunnel when magically a cab stopped in front of them, so they got in. At that exact moment, the tunnel, which had been completely closed to traffic except for emergency vehicles, reopened, and they were just about the very first car that was let through at about 1:45 p.m. They urged the cab driver, "Go as fast as you can and get us out of the city." The cab dropped them off in Queens, and one of Dennis's friends drove him home. When Dennis got home, there were lots of long hugs from his wife and two daughters, as well as from neighbors and friends.

Dennis worked for Blue Cross Blue Shield whose corporate headquarters were on the 16th through 26th floors of the North Tower. They had 1,600 employees there that tragic day. Sadly, thirteen innocent souls from Blue Cross Blue Shield did not make it out. It is believed that eleven were lost while on the elevator, and two were lost as they stayed behind. The two employees who stayed behind were a quadriplegic and his best friend; you may recall hearing this story on the news. The two friends, one in a special wheelchair to get around, waited until they could get down the staircase with help from the firemen. They never made it out.

To this day, Eleanor Andersen, the staff member who was having the argument with Dennis in his office that tragic morning, thanks him every time she sees him for saving her life. Her normal morning routine was to go up to the cafeteria on one of the upper floors at 8:30 a.m. to get coffee and a bagel. It was shortly after that time, at 8:46 a.m., that the 767 commercial jet plane hit the Tower she was in. Instead of going for her usual breakfast that morning, Eleanor was in Dennis's office arguing with him… on the 24th floor. If she had gone for coffee that morning, she believes she would never have made it out.

For me personally, in addition to the memories of anger, rage, and fear, I will never forget Robin's compassionate and generous offer of her Manhattan apartment for Dennis that night. Amid that great tragedy, there were so many heroic people and simple acts of kindness.

15

A Second Nightmare

It was about a month after September 11th, and the world was trying to get back to their daily lives. Back at PCH, we were trying to get back to running a business, especially with our long legal ordeal settled just a few months earlier. At this point, we were struggling to get out of the red when another nightmare occurred – a second debilitating threat to PCH and the entire direct marketing community – *white powder.*

A Second Nightmare

It was early October 2001, and three people in Florida were exposed to anthrax, likely from a letter or a parcel. One died within a few days from anthrax inhalation, an extremely rare and lethal disease, and the other two individuals were being treated. All three were employees of American Media Inc. which publishes magazines and supermarket tabloids, such as *The Sun* and *The National Enquirer.* The man who died was Bob Stevens, a photo editor at *The Sun.*

The FBI sealed off the entire office building where this took place, and all 300 employees who worked in the building were tested for anthrax. The country learned that inhalation anthrax is frighteningly 90% fatal.

There had been two disturbing incidents about a week earlier. A letter addressed to anchorman Tom Brokaw of *NBC Nightly News* was opened by his assistant who had contracted a different form of anthrax.

At about the same time, a letter containing a powdery substance was received by *The New York Times*, and that letter was also being tested.

Shortly after these initial incidents occurred, the FBI reported that it had received hundreds of hoaxes and was investigating all reports. During a briefing in Washington, D.C., Attorney General John Ashcroft told the public, "If individuals receive mail of which they are suspicious, they should not open it, they should not shake it," and he advised Americans to leave the area where they found such mail and call law enforcement and public health authorities.

Every consumer was concerned, and rightly so, about his or her own mail, especially since the September 11th terrorist attack of just one month prior raised fears of biological warfare. Needless to say, the response to all direct mail, including PCH's, nosedived during this period. We were already in a very weakened position. This couldn't have come at a worse time.

White Powder at PCH Headquarters

We put in heightened security measures at our Port Washington headquarters, as most companies did, and encouraged our printers, paper manufacturers, and lettershops around the country to do the same.

A week or so later, in late October, during the height of the anthrax alerts, we got our very own scare right in our own corporate headquarters. Some of the product returns from our customers were processed here, and one of the returned parcels – with white powder spilling out of it – was lying on the floor. This was exactly what anthrax was supposed to look like.

The parcel and the white powder were right in the middle of the building, in the midst of lots of employees, and yards from all the executive offices. A couple of VP's, including me, were called to attend to the situation. When I got there, the area had already been cordoned off. We gathered near the area, but left the parcel untouched, just lying there on the floor, surrounded by white powder. No one really knew what to do.

We were all thinking that we probably shouldn't even be near the cordoned off area. We quickly called one of our fulfillment managers to help us assess the situation. He speculated that the white powder might be a stain remover we sold called OxiClean, but unless he got closer to the spilled product, which he surely wouldn't do, this was but a guess. We discussed whether we should evacuate the building, but we decided not to.

We called the police and health authorities, and after a few terrifying hours, we determined that the parcel came from a good PCH customer. We conjectured that this meant that it was not likely to be anthrax. A few hours later, we got confirmation that the spilled substance was, in fact, OxiClean.

After Anthrax

The anthrax scare lasted several months and then fortunately subsided. During this timeframe, the consumers' response to all direct mail promotions around the country was reduced, including at PCH, so we were getting more and more worried by the day about our survival.

By 2002, PCH's future was still in doubt. We had managed to improve profitability to around breakeven, but we needed to do better than that to survive. One more downturn, even a small one, and that would be the end of Publishers Clearing House. It was up to the great PCH talent to put us back in the black.

16   The Great PCH Talent

I am happy to report – the skill and talent at PCH was finally able to pull us out of the deep hole we were in. With humility and respect, I can say that the people who worked at PCH were incredibly bright, creative, and resourceful. The synergy of working together contributed not only to our own accomplishments and ingenuity, but it also helped PCH to survive.

Direct marketing veteran Hank Rossi, with over forty years in the industry as owner of his own company, former executive at AOL, and top-notch consultant, said the following in reference to the PCH talent: "There is no question there were a lot of brilliant marketers working at PCH, and they achieved many things that were unbelievable when viewed by today's standards."

In case you feel bad for the PCH employees who lost their jobs, you shouldn't. The good news for our many laid-off employees was that with Publishers Clearing House on your resume, doors opened for you. It was like having a degree from Harvard or Yale. Even the PCH website acknowledges this fact by declaring: "Not surprisingly many direct marketing industry leaders learned their craft within the walls of the company known as PCH."

Virtually all former PCH employees went on to have highly successful careers. Many became key executives at other companies, and some even became CEO's or owners of their very own thriving businesses. Some of the well-known companies infused with PCH talent included

American Express, Time Inc., AOL, Barnes & Noble, 1-800-Flowers, *Newsweek*, and top advertising agencies like Ogilvy & Mather, Leo Burnet, and KSL Media.

The ensuing few stories from PCH's past, as well as my own, should lend some credence to how great the talent was at PCH.

Steve Juhasz

One small example of the PCH expertise is a story told to me by the highly regarded industry veteran Steve Juhasz, who worked at PCH for ten years.

Steve left PCH in the mid-1980's to work for a much larger company, Scandinavian Airlines, the largest airline in Scandinavia with over 25,000 employees. At PCH, Steve had been in charge of some of the smaller profit centers, and even though he never completed his college education, he learned all he needed from PCH.

When Steve was presenting his first business plan to the top management team at Scandinavian Airlines, their top brass was utterly astonished at the comprehensive and logical nature of his presentation and plan. His new bosses looked at him like he was a genius, but all he did was to write a business plan similar to the ones he was taught to do back at PCH.

Steve was stunned by the accolades of his new bosses, especially since he was often reprimanded and his work criticized by the demanding PCH Executive team. Today, Steve is a highly successful independent consultant, helping many companies with their production needs. He attributes his good fortune to his early education at Publishers Clearing House.

The Secret Challenge

Another example of the effectiveness of the PCH skill comes from the time we hired some outside experts to probe whether they could outperform our internal staff's methodology for our sophisticated name selection process.

When I first started working at PCH, the method we used to decide which customers would receive each of our mailings was quite simplistic. We used just three variables from a customer's past history with PCH. One variable was the customer's "frequency," that is, how often the customer had ordered in the past. The other two variables were "recency" and "monetary value." These three variables were used to determine how often a customer should be mailed, whether once a year, many times a year, or somewhere in between. The decisions on which customers to mail were the responsibility of the Marketing Analysis group.

In the late 1970's, we started to get much more sophisticated with respect to our name selection for our mailings. We speculated that if we used a lot more information about our customers, it would produce more profitable results. To accomplish this, my boss Bruce Pantano and I introduced a new group we named the "Statistical Development department." In lay terms, we would now use hundreds of variables pertaining to each customer's history instead of just three, and the customer selections would be done by skilled Statisticians who would use a technique called "statistical regression modeling." The end result was much more profitable customer mailings.

By the 1990's, due to our increased number of mailings, this new department grew to almost a dozen highly specialized, very well-paid professional employees, most of whom had Master's degrees in Statistics. Our Statisticians used dozens of different regression models depending on the situation, and they were responsible for deciding which customers were mailed in the numerous customer mailings each year. The department was managed by two first-rate Statisticians, Jamie Brown and Keith Bergendorf. For many years they analyzed, tweaked, and enhanced the department's modeling techniques, in addition to training a dedicated staff of Statisticians. None of what they did was really understood by senior management, but there was no doubt about the effectiveness of their work, as seen in the results of our mailings.

One day during our downsizing period, I was called into our President's office and asked whether I thought an outside specialist could do a better job with our name selection than our home-grown group of Statisticians. At this point in time, there was a very respected company, David Shepard Associates, who were experts at statistical modeling, and many companies had started to outsource their work to them. Our President knew David Shepard, who spoke at all the direct marketing industry functions, and who was known to have assembled an impressive group of Statisticians to work in his company – all with impressive Doctorate degrees in Statistics.

I wanted to say, "There is no way they can beat our talent." But I knew my opinion wouldn't matter in this instance, and that the top brass had already decided what needed to be done. So I replied that I had the utmost respect for our team of Statisticians, especially the two managers in the department, but that it certainly couldn't hurt to put together a test to see who could do a better job. As expected, we proceeded to test whether David Shepard's team could outdo our own home-grown staff.

I was never told this, but I knew exactly what the underlying challenge was for our Statistical Development group. Although we had already had several phases of downsizing, we were still losing money. If David Shepard Associates could do better – or even equal to – our own internal PCH staff, then we could eliminate more PCH employees, and we could realize more cost savings.

I knew that we needed to beat the outside specialists, or our entire Statistical Development team would be eliminated. Of course, I never said anything about this possible outcome to the managers or staff in the department, and I don't believe that anyone from the department fully realized what was at stake.

I didn't like it, but I fully understood that we needed to try everything in our power to lower costs and/or improve results. It would be sad if we needed to eliminate our home-grown talent, but when you are losing money, there is no choice but to leave no stone unturned.

Over the next month, one of David Shepard's most experienced employees with, of course, impeccable PhD credentials, perfected a regression model for the test. We used one of the newest programs at PCH, the Continuity program, to give David Shepard's company the best chance for success. The test involved taking random samples and mailing the group of customers selected by David Shepard's expert and separately mailing a second group selected by a PCH staff member, then comparing the actual results.

I waited anxiously for about two months for the results to come in. I will admit that even I was a bit surprised by the outcome. The test indicated that the work by our own Statisticians vastly outperformed the outside expert's effort. On the one hand, that was a big relief. On the other hand, however, if we could have dramatically improved the bottom line by outsourcing, I would have been all for it.

Now I don't believe this test result should be viewed as a slight to the David Shepard group. It is just a testament to how good we were at what we did at PCH. Over the years, David Shepard Associates has prospered, and today, they continue to have a team of highly seasoned professionals who provide a wide range of services to Fortune 500 companies in many industries as well as smaller niche players.

Do Dead People Respond to Junk Mail?

We knew that our direct mail copy was compelling, and as mentioned before, we tested everything imaginable. But no one expected this result.

From time to time at PCH, we would receive a letter that the person we mailed was deceased. We didn't like when this happened, and when it did, we quickly responded by taking the name off our customer list. We didn't find this situation surprising because we were mailing so many customers. At one point, though, we thought that perhaps we should be more proactive. We could go out and purchase, or rent, an outside list of deceased individuals and match them to our customer list in order to eliminate all matches from our mailing. Our customer file was so very large, at over 40 million, that there would certainly be some hits with an external list of deceased names.

This whole area was extraordinarily sensitive, to say the least. We had two serious concerns. First, we certainly didn't want the outside world – that is, the press – to misinterpret our intentions. After the press had completely misinterpreted and blew out of proportion the handful of sweepstakes entries that had been found discarded, who knows what they would say if they heard we were buying lists of dead people? Second, we didn't really know how accurate the outside sources were in compiling lists of deceased individuals.

We all agreed, however, that it was not a good idea to mail someone who wasn't alive. So guess what we did. In typical PCH fashion, we tested it. We rented for one-time use only an external list of deceased individuals and matched this outside list to our customer file. Any matches were flagged and mailed in their regularly scheduled mailing. We fully expected response to be very low, and that would prove to us that we should be more proactive than we already were.

To our surprise, however, it turned out that the matches actually had an above average response rate and were profitable to mail. We concluded that there must be other people in the household responding to our promotion. That's how powerful our copy was. Based on this result, we decided not to proceed with this highly sensitive effort.

Merchandise Is Introduced

The marketing of products other than magazines was one reason for our astounding growth in the 1980's and 1990's. Merchandise was first introduced in 1985 with one or two products but soon expanded to a wide range of items, from books, music, videos and DVDs, to kitchen gadgets, household items, jewelry, horticulture, food, collectibles, and more.

One of the most successful products, early on, was the Hershey's Chocolate Cookbook. It had an incredible cover shot of an absolutely delectable looking homemade chocolate cake. The first time we promoted it, the result shocked us all. It broke all records at PCH and was by far the biggest seller in the mailing. We sold enough of these cookbooks to make it a best seller many times over. It was this cookbook's initial impressive result that encouraged PCH to start promoting more non-magazine products in our mailings.

What was amusing about this result was what the exact same customers bought two weeks later. We happened to have a diet cookbook in a subsequent mailing, and the diet book was the top seller – to the same customers who had just bought the chocolate cookbook. We joked, first fatten them up, then tell them they need to lose weight.

Another really big early seller at PCH was the Richard Simmons' exercise video, *Sweatin' to the Oldies*. We sold so many of these videos that the nation's foremost exercise expert came out to Publishers Clearing House one day to thank us. Richard Simmons ran frenetically up and down the PCH hallways, roamed in and out of many of the offices, and greeted all the PCH employees he could find. He bounded around PCH smiling and hugging everyone. In person, he is just like he is on television… an uncontrollable tornado. It was the dead of winter and snowing the day he came out to PCH, but he still wore his trademark tiny shorts and brightly colored, skimpy tank top.

Consulting

The final example of how great the training was at PCH and how skilled we were at what we did concerns the part-time consulting I did after I left PCH. When I retired at a young age at the end of 2002, I had no thoughts of ever going back to work. However, after three enjoyable and relaxing years of being fully retired, I became a little bored. This probably had something to do with my twin daughters leaving for college soon and my wife and I becoming what they call "empty nesters." At this point I decided to try some limited part-time consulting.

I knew that what I had learned at PCH over those thirty years was invaluable, and I looked forward to using what I had learned. However, there was still some lingering doubt in my mind about how effective my knowledge would be. It had been three years since I had had any contact with the business world or the direct marketing community. I also was not 100% sure how much my PCH experience, and especially those thousands of test results, would hold up if I were to get an assignment in a non-sweepstakes medium.

I got my first consulting job in 2006, and I drew on all my PCH experience. The assignment was almost perfect for me; it came from a small but very reputable magazine publisher called MediZine. I got this assignment after meeting with their President, Traver Hutchins, and their Chairman, Dale Lang. It turned out that Dale was a long time publisher himself, and he knew many of the old-time, gifted PCH executives and former colleagues of mine.

My new prospective client was enamored with my PCH background, but both executives questioned me about whether my experience would

translate to their environment – non-sweepstakes and the pharmaceutical field. I replied to them, confidently and with complete conviction
that, "Human behavior is human behavior, and the test results at PCH
would surely be the same elsewhere." I really did believe this, and testing
in different and unique marketplaces at PCH had shown this to be true,
but there was still some lingering self-doubt in my mind.

Mr. Hutchins and Mr. Lang were very concerned about missing their
circulation rate base and wanted my help to improve their direct mail
copy so they could make their numbers by year-end. We agreed on a
short-term assignment that would take three to four weeks, and my job
was to suggest improvements to their creative and marketing activities.
During the discussion about the assignment, I informed MediZine's
President, "I am not a writer, but I will tell your staff what to write." He
agreed with that approach, and we struck a deal in which my fee would
be paid half up front and the other half only if I could improve their
order response by 25% or more. This was a fair arrangement for both
of us, although I imagine that MediZine thought there was no way the
second part of my fee would come into play.

I made my recommendations, and they loved my suggestions, so
they decided to implement the copy changes immediately. They also
back-tested the old copy so they could determine the value of the
changes.

I remember estimating that the copy changes should improve their
order response by around 50%, so I figured that even if the changes
were only half as effective as I thought, I would still earn the second
part of my fee. But I said to myself, what did I really know? This was
a non-sweepstakes publisher and in the pharmaceutical industry. That
self-doubt reared its ugly head again!

I was new at consulting, so before I had made my recommendations I met with a former business colleague who had been successfully
consulting full-time for many years. I asked him if he thought I should
indicate to my client that I expected a 50% improvement due to my direct mail copy changes. He replied emphatically, "Absolutely not!" My
veteran colleague didn't believe I could get that kind of improvement.
And he went on to say that even if I could achieve that result, the client

would then expect it. I agreed with his thinking and didn't tell the client my prediction.

I patiently and confidently waited the few months it took for the test results to come in. When I finally received the awaited email from MediZine about the test results, that ugly self-doubt reappeared yet again, and I was afraid to open it. I stared at my email inbox for a few minutes, then slowly and reluctantly clicked, "Open." The very brief message gave me a huge sense of accomplishment. It simply said, "The changes were a huge success – test increased order response overall by 55%."

I could not believe how accurate my assessment had been! I thought to myself, "Those thirty years at PCH really taught me well!" I was thrilled and so was MediZine. They made their rate base, and I earned the second half of my consulting fee.

For me, this result validated my thirty years of hard work at a re-markable company. It was heartening to see how valuable my time at PCH had been. It wasn't just that I had earned the second part of my consulting fee. It meant much, much more… and it reaffirms how great the training, experience, and talent were at PCH.

As of the writing of this book, I continue to do some limited part-time consulting. But I certainly don't want it to interfere too much with my retirement.

PCH Winner Stories

Part 2

What Happens When No One Is Home?
K. J. Macalister ($10 million)

In January 1998, after flawlessly executing a live telecast on the Super Bowl post-game show for a few years in a row, a winner wasn't home. This was the risk the Prize Patrol faced with each live broadcast, and was something that Dave and Todd always feared. Somehow, the detailed, undercover detective work done by the Prize Patrol came up short that year.

The live TV commercial started from outside the apartment building where the winner lived with three longtime friends. Video cameras then followed the Prize Patrol inside as they raced down the long hallway, but their pleading knocks on the door went unanswered. "Guess our winner isn't home," Dave told Todd and millions of television viewers in the live TV commercial. The Prize Patrol team was then shown hanging a giant sign on the door knob that said, "While You Were Out…" This was the Prize Patrol's back-up plan if this situation ever occurred.

Kathy-Jo Macalister, or K. J. as she is known to family and friends, was found about two hours later, after the live broadcast had already aired. K. J., a twenty-two year old college student, was at her boyfriend's home at the time playing video games. In hindsight and to our surprise, it turned out that the winner not being home was not such a bad thing after all. It showed the skeptics that PCH winners were not notified ahead of time or part of a staged presentation.

Three days after her win, K. J. flew to Amarillo, Texas, with eight of her closest friends where she gave her first national TV interview on *The Oprah Winfrey Show*. K. J. revealed that her plans were to complete her education and to take a trip. She said, "Now I can tour the world. I was going to do that anyway, but this just makes it a better trip."

Friday the 13th Winner – Artis Eldridge ($1 million)

Ms. Eldridge was born on an unlucky day but her luck was about to change. She lived on California's Mojave Desert and her rough upbringing didn't phase this remarkable woman. In her modest desert home also lived two elderly ladies who probably would have been homeless, but Artis took them in as their caretaker. Unfortunately, Artis's finances were not in great shape and she had recently filed for bankruptcy in order to save her home.

Her million dollar surprise in August 1989 made her life a whole lot easier. But when Artis was invited to New York to celebrate her good fortune, she refused because she couldn't leave her two frail housemates. So Dave Sayer took Artis and her two wheelchair bound, elder companions to Disneyland. When Dave met them in the parking lot, he was immediately struck by her strong personality. Artis commanded Dave, "You push one wheelchair and I'll push the other."

Oldest Winner

In 2004, the Prize Patrol delivered a $25,000 check to a retired Wichita couple who had been married for more than fifty years. When asked what they were going to do with the money, the ninety-one year old husband replied that they would put the money away for a rainy day. Now that's an optimist!

Farthest Winner

The Prize Patrol delivered one prize by dogsled to a winner in a remote town in Alaska. No black van this time, just a very long ride on a dogsled. I can tell you that Dave and Todd don't want to repeat this snowy adventure. In fact, when PCH awards its big prize every January, I know for a fact that Dave and Todd are always hoping for someplace warm and exotic… like Hawaii.

Smelliest Winner

Dave Sayer doesn't like to talk about this particular trip – to a pig farm in the Midwest – and you won't see this adventure in any of our TV commercials either. If you have ever been to a real pig farm, and I have, you would know why. The stench can kill you. I don't know if our winner kept all his hogs or not after his big win.

Other adventures Dave doesn't like to talk about are his close call with two unfriendly pit bulls, and then there was the time he had a run-in with the police while staking out a winner's home. It's a good thing Dave is unflappable. It certainly has helped him with the many unique situations he's been in.

Biggest PCH Prize Winner
Ginny Jackson ($21 million)

Ginny Jackson from Abilene, Texas, won the largest prize ever awarded by PCH. A whopping $21 million on Super Bowl Sunday, January 2000.

Ginny Jackson thought a caravan of strangers pulling their cars into her driveway on Super Bowl Sunday was lost. A stunned Ginny later told reporters, "I thought someone had gotten lost and stopped here for directions." Her home was right off the highway and at the end of a gravel road, so she was used to being approached by strangers.

Soon after the surprise, her husband Jack came rushing home from her brother's house, where he had gone to watch the Super Bowl. Ginny told him she kept expecting someone to jump out and say it was all a big joke, but Dave Sayer made it all believable when he handed her a check for $250,000, the first installment of her big prize. Dave also informed her that along with the $21 million, she had a choice between a Lincoln Towncar, a Lincoln Navigator, or $50,000 cash. She went for the Navigator; she didn't really need the cash anymore.

Ginny's plans for the windfall were to help her kids finish college and give some to her church. Her husband, on the other hand, had other plans. He told reporters he would "shave, put on a suit and tie, and go into hiding, because nobody would recognize me if I do that." That was his solution to avoiding all the unwanted new friends he was about to get.

Most Timely Win – Stephanie Gornichec ($1 million)

On the verge of bankruptcy and forced to sell their home in Caldwell, Iowa, this windfall couldn't have come at a better time. Stephanie Gornichec had lost her job about a year earlier, and she and her husband were about to sell their home to make ends meet. The very first thing Stephanie did after she was told she won $1 million was to defiantly take down the "For Sale" sign in front of their home.

A few months later, in October 2009, Stephanie went on *The Oprah Winfrey Show* to tell Oprah and her viewers all about her experience with the famous Prize Patrol. In the meantime, Oprah had a surprise of her own for her Chicago studio audience that day. And back at PCH headquarters, our employees knew something special was planned because they were all invited to watch *Oprah* in the cafeteria.

Stephanie described to Oprah and her audience how she had been surprised by the Prize Patrol. When she was done, the PCH Prize Patrol van, from out of nowhere, drove right onto Oprah's stage. Dave and Todd then popped out of the van with a giant check in hand. They announced to the shocked crowd that audience member Sue Draper was a winner of $25,000. Sue was all smiles as she dashed onstage to collect her PCH prize.

At the end of the show, to make sure everyone left happy, there was one more surprise. The Prize Patrol announced that everyone in the studio audience had won $500 cash. Oprah's audience went wild!

Most Skeptical Winner – David Koobs ($10 million)

PCH had difficulty contacting David Koobs in advance to secretly plan out his surprise. The Prize Patrol called and left David messages, but he thought they were prank calls, so he didn't return the calls. Not knowing what to do, the Prize Patrol found out where David worked and planned to surprise him at the Miami, Florida hospital where he was employed as an anesthesiologist. What the Prize Patrol didn't know was that David was going to be busy when they showed up.

When the Prize Patrol arrived in January 1991, David was in the Operating Room. Thankfully for the patient, David refused to come to the lobby until after the operation was over. As David emerged from the Operating Room in his green hospital scrubs, the Prize Patrol was there to record the event. It still took some convincing to get the skeptical David to believe that he had really won ten million big ones.

In typical fashion, we invited our winner to visit PCH along with his fiancée and her two sons. The entire PCH staff was there to greet them in the cafeteria. David couldn't stop smiling, but his fiancée and the boys, who were less accustomed to the fanfare, looked like they were in shock.

Thirty Winners in Thirty Days

Surprising thirty winners in just one month's time had great promotional and commercial appeal. This new idea proposed by Todd Sloane sounded great in theory, but was it possible? The truth is we really didn't know if we could pull this off, but in true PCH fashion, we were going to try.

To accomplish this implausible feat, we would elicit help from PCH employees by making them temporary Prize Patrol team members. The plan was to train them on how to deliver and record the surprise, which would enable us to surprise that many winners in so short a time. The promotion was called "*Wake Up a Winner for a Month*" and prizes ranged from $1,000 to $100,000.

The first obstacle was the ever-increasing workload for all of us at PCH. Who would have the time to go to the training, let alone take the three days required to complete the assignment? But we didn't let this dilemma stop us and finally settled on sixty-four volunteers.

Dave and Todd did the training at PCH headquarters, and it was dubbed, "The Prize Patrol Boot Camp." The training was serious but, of course, loads of fun at the same time. The new Prize Patrol team members, whom we called "Prize Patrol Deputies," were being prepared to go out in teams of two, and:

- Investigate where the winner lived,

- Make the necessary flight and hotel reservations,

- Take along blue blazers with the PCH patch embossed on it,

- Learn how to handle a small video camera so the winning moment could be recorded,

- Rent a black van at the local airport,

- Once at the destination, apply the large PCH emblem to the side of the van and buy flowers, balloons, and champagne,

- Find the winner, and then, and most importantly,…

- Be ready for anything!!!

To get the training right, we installed a mock front door in one of the large conference rooms at PCH headquarters. Experienced Prize Patrol members stood behind the door while the deputies-in-training took turns knocking on the door. Different winner scenarios would be played out. The Prize Patrol needed to be ready for anything.

This promotional event was a modest success, although it took an incredible amount of blood, sweat, and tears from quite a number of employees. There were plenty of fun adventures to be told when the Prize Patrol deputies came home. Some were joyful stories, like the time the local florist got so excited about the escapade that the storekeeper actually closed up shop to go along with the Prize Patrol. Other adventures were not so happy, like the time one of our teams got stuck in a swamp.

From time to time, PCH has repeated similar events, such as a promotion in 2009 where we awarded 101 prizes in 101 zip codes across the country. This was accomplished in a miraculous three-day timeframe with over sixty Prize Patrol deputies.

Coldest Winner – Beata Sankiewicz ($10 million)

It can get cold in late January, but especially when you are in Canada's Sudbury, Ontario. The Prize Patrol team had to wait in minus 20-degree temperature for what seemed like an eternity until our $10 million winner opened her door on that frigid Super Bowl Sunday in 1997.

From the very first moment the Prize Patrol met Beata, it was obvious that her trip to New York for our Winners Weekend was going to be more of a challenge than usual. Beata was from Poland, and she spoke very little English. She invited her boyfriend to join her for the trip to New York, which was fine with us, but he also didn't speak much English, so we looked for an interpreter. It just so happened that we found one in our very own PCH Controller, Ted Kasnicki. Both of Ted's parents were from Poland.

At lunch Ted and Beata enjoyed speaking Polish together, and Ted spent the entire day translating for her. Ted could hear and understand the winner's private conversations and whispers with her boyfriend, and it soon became clear to Ted that our winner's boyfriend wanted to get married. Ted thought the boyfriend appeared a bit too eager about Beata's newfound wealth. And apparently so did Beata, who seemed to be having second thoughts about marrying her companion. Ten million dollars can do that to you! I am not sure if they ever got married or not.

Winner at 36,000 Feet

In early 2001, the Prize Patrol boarded an Atlanta-to-Los Angeles flight and at 36,000 feet surprised the winner with a $100,000 prize. The winner was a lucky grandmother on her way to a family reunion.

The flight crew was in on the surprise and helped the Prize Patrol sneak on board. The winner was surprised somewhere over Texas, and in spite of the tight quarters, the Prize Patrol presented the winner with balloons, champagne, and the oversized check. Everyone cheered the new winner, and the stunned reaction was, of course, captured on videotape for use in a PCH TV commercial.

Our Fiftieth PCH Millionaire
Elizabeth Green ($1 million)

On February 28, 2009, PCH made eighty-one year old Elizabeth Green of Sparta, Tennessee, our fiftieth winner of $1 million or more. Her surprise award was televised in a live commercial seen on *NBC Nightly News with Brian Williams*.

Mrs. Green was initially informed that she had won a $1,000 prize. What she didn't know was that she was soon to become the richest farmer in White County. Mrs. Green's first thought after being told she won $1,000 was that now she could afford to buy enough fertilizer to cover her fields. She was unprepared when the Prize Patrol arrived with roses, balloons, champagne, and a bigger check.

With her bigger win, Mrs. Green said that she planned on taking care of her two children, five grandchildren and three great-grandchildren, and also to donate some of her winnings to the St. Jude Children's Hospital. She had been entering for years and said, "I didn't want to tell anyone 'cause I thought they'd make fun of me." I guarantee you, no one is making fun of her now.

Busiest Winner – Natalie Bostelman ($1 million)

Natalie Bostelman, from Toledo, Ohio, was working three jobs at the time, so it was no surprise that the Prize Patrol found her at work in August 2008. When Natalie was shown the big check, she collapsed to the floor with a scream and then started chanting over and over and over again, "I won a million dollars. I won a million dollars. I won a million dollars."

Natalie was looking forward to reducing her workload, and she and her husband were going to start building her dream house on a large piece of property where their mobile home stood.

The Luckiest Husband – Pearl Cooper ($100,000)

In the 1970's, Pearl Cooper's husband was a typical skeptic. When he saw the Publishers Clearing House promotional mailing piece one day, he immediately tossed it into the garbage. Fortunately for Mr. Cooper, later that day his wife Pearl noticed the sweepstakes package in the garbage can. She quickly took it out of the garbage and entered the PCH contest. It was the best decision she ever made, as that was the winning entry for the top prize in the PCH sweepstakes that year.

We flew Pearl and her lucky husband in for Winners Weekend in New York for the usual fanfare. We showed them around the Big Apple and presented their prize in front of a large audience at PCH headquarters.

Mr. Cooper was especially jovial about his wife's actions... and I don't think he will ever question her judgment again.

Good As Gold Awards

In 1993, PCH initiated something new – a program we called the "Good As Gold Awards" where PCH recognized other kinds of winners. The idea came from Dave Sayer, who said, "Too bad we couldn't give more to those people who do such good things for the community." Senior management listened and put his words into action.

Each year, PCH contacted about 2,000 media outlets across the country and requested they submit stories of local volunteers for the award, looking for unsung heroes who rendered outstanding service to their community. Each year, ten deserving individuals were selected by an impartial panel from nominees submitted by the media. Each honoree was then surprised in typical PCH tradition with an unannounced visit from the Prize Patrol, and each received a crystal and gold trophy, plus $10,000 in cash. Of course, in addition to our good intentions and philanthropic spirit, we hoped this would lead to some positive press about PCH.

Since its inception, almost one hundred "Good As Gold Awards" have been given out. Interestingly, I was told that the judging was a real challenge because there were so many deserving people who did wonderful things for their communities. That was nice to hear, especially when most of the news is about violence, corruption, and the like.

One such winner was Carolyn Piraino of Oakland, California, a teacher who truly cared. Carolyn noticed that many of her students were showing up at the nurse's office every Monday morning with stomachaches. In this school district, the needy children were provided free hot meals during school, but some were not eating well, or at all, over the weekends. Carolyn decided to try to help and went to local businesses to see if they would provide food bags that the young students could take home with them over the weekend. She called it the "Children's Food Basket." Her program was so successful that it was soon expanded to schools in the surrounding areas as well.

A second example was Flo Wheatley from a small town outside of Scranton, Pennsylvania. She won her $10,000 award on *The Montel Williams Show* for her introduction of a program she called "My Brother's Keeper Quilt Group." Flo took her favorite pastime, sewing, and turned it into a lifesaving project for thousands of homeless people nationwide. Flo and her volunteers made sleeping bags sewn from everything from old blue jeans to scraps of material and distributed them to the homeless across the country. Her motivation was inspired by a homeless man in New York City who helped her and her ailing son out of a jam one day. As Flo tells the story, they were on their way home from her young son's daily cancer treatments. Her son was near collapse, but commuters just rushed past them, when a homeless man said, "You need help, lady." The homeless man then picked up her suitcase and got on the subway with them. They all got off at Flo's station and the homeless man hailed them a taxi. Flo gave the homeless man $5 for helping her, and the man said to her, softly, "Don't abandon me." Flo never forgot those words. To date, more than 100,000 sleeping bags or quilts have been distributed to homeless people and shelters in Manhattan and other large cities.

These are just two of many examples of our Good As Gold Award winners. This program continued for seven or eight years, but sadly, it was one of the casualties of our many cost-cutting measures. I don't believe it has since been reinstated.

18

The Fun We Had

|||||||||||||||||||||||||||||||||||||||||||||||||||||||||||||||||||||||||||||||||||||||||||||||||||||||||||||||||||||||

Some Personal Stories

Now that you've read about the true inside story of PCH, our contest winners, and the Mertz family, I'll share some personal PCH stories that I know you will enjoy. They reveal the camaraderie, adventure, fun, and spirit we all embraced and loved about PCH and our fellow employees.

Co-Worker and I Get Our Boss Fired... and Almost Kill a Spectator

I had been at PCH for only about two years when a new boss was hired to manage the small but growing Marketing Analysis department. At the time, the department consisted of myself, three other Marketing Analysts, a secretary, and a few full-time clerical workers. Our new boss, an older gentleman, was hired by Vice President Alan Rabinowitz. After a few months on the job, it became clear to us that our new boss was completely ineffective. To add insult to injury, he was also not working as hard as the rest of us.

One of my co-workers convinced me that we had to discuss this situation with Alan. We secretly talked about how to approach him, knowing this would not be an enjoyable meeting. After much debate, we agreed that the best way to handle it was to invite Alan out for a drink after work. So we sent Alan a note, just saying that the two of us wanted to have a private conversation with him outside the office. Alan responded by setting up a meeting for the following week at 7:00 p.m. at Rothman's Steak House. This was the perfect place for a nice private conversation; in addition, it was a half hour away so we wouldn't run into anyone else from PCH. We hadn't told Alan what we wanted to talk about, and he didn't ask.

My colleague and I were quite nervous about this meeting. We arrived a half hour early and had two quick drinks each to calm our nerves. When Alan arrived, he promptly ordered his favorite drink, an extra dry martini, and asked us what we wanted to drink. Trying to look like mature adults, we both replied we would have the same. Alan quickly downed his first martini and ordered another. My cohort and I followed his lead and got a second martini as well. These were my first two martinis ever, and I think the same was true for my colleague. By this time, my partner-in-crime and I were completely plastered. We both had four drinks in about one hour's time; it didn't help that we hadn't had anything to eat. Alan, meanwhile, could hold his liquor, had far less than we did, and was stone sober.

We told Alan our thoughts about the new boss he had hired. We were surprised that Alan listened to us rather intently. Of course, we were hiding our "drunkenness," or at least trying to. Alan had a couple of questions about the situation, and then said he would think about what we talked about. With the meeting over, Alan left.

At this point, my business colleague and I could barely walk, so we decided to have a bite to eat. We proceeded to get a table at this very fine, upscale restaurant and ordered some big juicy steaks. This is one of those elegant establishments that provides the diners with a giant Jim Bowie style knife to cut your steak. As we were eating, my friend's knife somehow slipped out of her hand and flew onto the table next to us. I am not really sure how this happened, but it did. There were four people at the next table, and the oversized knife almost stabbed one of them. Thoroughly mortified, we embarrassingly retrieved the knife, glad that no one got hurt.

A few days later, our new boss was suddenly gone. Alan called us to thank us for our honest feedback. I am sure he must have noticed how tipsy we were that evening, but he never mentioned it.

Skinny Dipping

Please don't tell this story to my former boss, Bruce Pantano, because I know he wouldn't approve. Just kidding! Bruce is a great friend, mentor, and confidant. I reported to him for many years, including during his tenure as President of PCH. I know Bruce would not approve of employees skinny-dipping during business hours, but I found out that my mid-day adventure was a great way to reinvigorate oneself. I don't think, however, that it will catch on in the business world.

It was a fairly typical day at the office. I was in very early and busy working, trying to keep up with the challenging and ever-increasing workload. One of my best friends, Dean Stephens, who lived in town, called me. Dean had his days free because he worked at night managing a restaurant and bar, and he suggested we go out to lunch. I agreed, as I had many times in the past, and we met at our favorite local restaurant, The Clubhouse.

We had an enjoyable lunch and were just finishing dessert when Dean suggested, "Let's go enjoy the beautiful day, sit at my beach, and shoot the breeze." Dean's family owned a private, secluded plot of beach-front land in Sands Point, just a few minutes away. I had a lot of work to do and was hesitant, but my good friend could be very persuasive. I reluctantly agreed to spend just a bit more time away from my desk.

So, ten minutes later, there we were, sitting on this secluded, private, sandy beach. It was brutally hot, approaching 100 degrees when Dean urged, "Let's go for a swim." I was not prepared in any way to go swimming, and neither was Dean. Neither of us had towels, bathing trunks, or a change of clothes. But the heat was really getting to us. So we stripped down to our birthday suits and jumped in. It was, of course, extraordinarily refreshing. We talked, splashed each other, and hopped around like kids without a care in the world. After about fifteen minutes, we got out of the cool, refreshing water.

Since we had no towels, and we didn't want to get sand all over us, we just stood there, like statues, in the hot sun to dry off. I must confess that when I got back to the office, it was probably one of the most productive days I ever had. I worked with a very big smile on my face that afternoon, and will never forget that extended lunch where two great friends left all their worries behind and acted like little boys again.

Like a Kid in a Candy Store

The business was growing so rapidly in the 1970's that we had trouble hiring enough temporary workers to process the massive number of incoming sweepstakes entries and orders we received. The peak periods were January and July, with January being the bigger of the two.

For our peak campaigns, we needed over 1,000 extra part-time employees to help process the mail, but hiring that many part-time workers in the small suburb of Port Washington was no simple task. Our Human Resource department did everything they could to find temporary workers, including running ads in all the local papers, posting ads at the local colleges, and asking PCH employees if they had relatives looking for a temporary assignment. The good news in finding that many temps was that most college kids were off from late December until mid-January and in the summer, which fortunately coincided with our peak periods. The skill set needed was minimal at best, as the temporary workers would simply be opening and sorting all the orders and non-orders, which would then either be scanned by our computers or sent to key entry for manual data entry. In the early days, we had only one building to hold all of the workers, our corporate headquarters in Port Washington.

These peak periods were chaotic at best. Margarete Thuemmler, a very intimidating German woman we fondly referred to as our "drill sergeant," was in charge of the organized chaos. Margarete worked at PCH for thirty-eight years, and underneath her strict demeanor was really a kind, devoted, caring lady. I think her thick German accent contributed to her ability to control the hundreds of temps. It didn't help, though, that the temporary workers were seated all together in large open areas, packed in like sardines. An added problem was that our parking lot didn't have anywhere near the space needed for that many extra cars, so we required all temps to park at a local park a few minutes away, and we bused them to and from work.

This whole situation made for some difficult and sometimes bizarre encounters. The temps were very closely watched and managed, especially since some of the envelopes that came in had cash in them. The only way to handle the large unruly group was to have many very strictly enforced rules. Margarete, our drill sergeant, was perfect for the job, and has many a story about her hordes of temps. Once, she enforced our strict parking rules and fired two temps for parking in the wrong place. Embarrassingly, it turned out that both were relatives of important PCH management. One was the nephew of one of our Human Resource Managers, and the other was the niece of a Vice President. Even in these cases we didn't make exceptions to the rules, and these two temps were let go. We felt that if we made exceptions, pure bedlam would ensue. The absolute worst offense, however, was when we had to walk one temp off the premises because he was masturbating on the envelopes he was opening. To make matters worse, this young man found his way back into the building so we had to walk him out twice.

The close-knit quarters for full-time and part-time employees created an environment where a lot of "playing around" took place, some ending in marriage and some not. They say that the attitude of a company comes from the top, and in our case, this may have been true. Our President after Lou Kislik was the highly charismatic John Mienik. John and his first wife divorced after John had a scandalous affair with his secretary, whom he subsequently married. Then many years later, John met Nancy Netke, a tall, slender, pretty woman at least twenty years his junior who worked in our Creative department. John divorced his second wife and married Nancy. I am sad to say that John passed away of a heart attack at a young age in spite of being fit and trim and a vegetarian.

Life at PCH in those early years, the '70's, was simply grand. At the time, I was in my late twenties and still single. We hired so many cute young part-time girls that I felt like a kid in a candy store. I will only say that for the first time in my life, I dated three women at the same time. I am not sure how I fit in the long work hours plus juggled three temporary-worker girlfriends, except to say I was very young. One of the three was a serious relationship, but there were complications. This was, of course, well before I met the love of my life, Rocey, my wonderful wife.

Trip to Paris

In 1990 I was offered the opportunity of a lifetime... an all expense paid trip to Paris, not just for myself, but for my wife as well. It would be a business trip for me and a sightseeing trip for her. The generous offer was made to a handful of PCH executives who had been helping our sister company in France. This company, France Abonnements, was partly owned by PCH and run by a very cordial Frenchman, Philippe Vigneron. The company was in the direct marketing business like PCH and used a similar sweepstakes promotion. Philippe had been coming to New York often, meeting with us and going over our latest test results. He would then take all he learned back to France.

For my wife and me, there was only one small problem. Actually, there were two small problems. My wife had given birth to twin girls a few months earlier, and the trip would be when our precious little girls were only four months old. If it had been up to me, we probably wouldn't have gone. But Rocey really wanted to go, and she sure could have used the break. France was a place my wife had always dreamed about visiting since she had studied French in school.

We couldn't count on our parents to help full-time because they were at the age where that wasn't an option. We did, however, know a really great live-in baby nurse, one who specialized in twins. We had hired this young woman, Judith, a registered nurse from Trinidad, to help us out for a few weeks when our girls were first born. So we proceeded to hire our former baby nurse, and enlisted my dad and stepmother plus both my brothers' families to help out as well. We were able to arrange it so there would be at least two people taking care of our cherished girls at any given time. With everything covered, we made plans for five days in Paris.

One week before the trip, however, our baby nurse called with some bad news – she had to cancel. She had been scheduled to care for another set of twins after our Paris trip, but they had arrived early, and she felt obligated to keep that engagement. Rocey and I agonized over whether we should cancel the trip. After much discussion, we decided to make the trip shorter, hired another nanny that we knew, and got the rest of the family to help out even more.

The trip to Paris was incredible. Our host, Philippe, treated us like royalty, including flowers in the hotel room when we arrived and sightseeing tours for the spouses. The side trips for Rocey included a trip to the historic and beautiful Palace of Versailles and an excursion to a very old countryside vineyard. One night we were all invited to have hors d'oeuvres and wine at Philippe's beautiful home, and then he took everyone out to dinner at the world famous *Maxim's de Paris*. My wife and I had a magical time, and we were especially appreciative towards our gracious host, but we also looked forward to getting home to see our little girls.

On our last day, we got to the airport as instructed at 6:00 a.m. sharp, two hours before the flight. As we were entering the airport, we noticed that it was completely deserted. It looked like there was a bomb scare and that they had evacuated the entire large complex. It was a very eerie feeling to be standing in the middle of a vast airport with absolutely nobody in sight. We waited at the unattended airline counter for several minutes until a flight attendant finally wandered over. She informed us that there was an air traffic controllers strike which had started that very morning and that our flight was now supposed to leave six hours late. That was a hellishly long six hours! Thankfully, the flight left exactly six hours late, as we were told. To this day, I hate going to the airport.

We got home and all was well, although to our disappointment, it didn't seem that either of our precious girls missed us in the slightest.

The Bribe

Every August, PCH hosted a company picnic at the local neighborhood park. Virtually everyone from Publishers Clearing House attended these functions, and I especially liked these events because they always included a barbeque. Truth be told, it was the only time all year that I got to eat meat due to my vegetarian wife. She is in charge of the meals, so at home, beef is never served. Whenever I would go to a barbeque, however, and especially if my wife wasn't there, I usually would give in to my taste buds. That once-a-year juicy charbroiled burger with melted cheese tastes like heaven. This was one of those occasions.

After one annual picnic, I arrived at work the very next day to find a large three-foot color poster leaning against my office door with a life-size close-up of me munching on a cheeseburger. The note attached to the poster said in large, block letters:

RANSOM NECESSARY OR PICTURE GOES TO YOUR VEGETARIAN WIFE.

Unbeknownst to me, someone had obviously taken a picture of me at the picnic. Many departments were reporting to me at the time, but I knew exactly who the culprits were. I also knew their price!

Early the next day, before anyone else arrived, I humbly dropped off two dozen fresh Crispy Crème doughnuts to the group responsible for the blackmail. Ransom paid and accepted! It was all in good fun, and we had a good laugh over it.

The Urn from the Ruins of Pompeii

This story was told to me by Tom Bass, who worked with the Mertz family in the early days.

It was the early 1960's, and the small handful of PCH employees was always helping out the Mertz family in one way or another. PCH had outgrown the Volkswagen van that was used to transfer printed material between buildings and deliver or pick up mail from the Post Office, and had just purchased a new, much larger truck. The new vehicle, an International Harvester Loadstar, was a good-sized truck such as the ones used for delivery of appliances.

At the time, Tom Bass was working part-time in the Lettershop department while also attending Adelphi University. His manager, John Dybus, asked him if he would like to work one Saturday, driving the new truck into New York City. At time-and-a-half, the $3/hour would come in handy for his tuition, so Tom agreed. After Tom gave this more consideration, though, he had second thoughts because he didn't have a Commercial Driver's License. Tom discussed this with his boss and was assured that he didn't need it, as this was the largest truck that one could drive without a commercial license at that time.

When Saturday came, Tom and a helper were told to go to the Pierre Apartments in Port Washington to pick up whatever the Mertzes wanted to bring to New York City. As it turned out, there wasn't really that much going to Manhattan – several boxes of things, a metal coat rack, and a very heavy, very large decorative urn that took two of them to lift. All told, they had only about a quarter of the truck utilized. Tom was concerned that the urn would topple over and roll around in the back of the truck and get broken, but they had no good way to secure the urn. So they put the metal coat rack on its side, stood the heavy urn upright, and wedged and supported the urn with the coat rack. Tom still had reservations about the urn's safety, but they had no other way to secure it.

They then embarked on the forty-five minute drive from the Long Island Expressway to the Midtown Tunnel. Back in the '60's this stretch of road was like a washboard, full of bumps and potholes. When they hit this highway, Tom's head was literally bouncing against the roof of the truck, especially since this was in the era before seatbelts. Tom couldn't help but fear that the urn was faring worse off in the back of the truck.

When they dropped off part of their load at Joyce Mertz's brownstone in downtown NYC, Tom couldn't believe the urn was still intact and standing upright. Apparently, it was so heavy, it didn't topple over. After this delivery, they went up to the Mertz's apartment at UN Plaza. On the way there, they encountered more potholes and some cobblestone sections of the street downtown. Again, Tom feared that the urn would end up in more than one piece. However, when they unloaded it at their apartment, it was fine and Tom breathed a big sigh of relief.

A couple days later, Tom was telling his boss John Dybus about their adventure delivering the Mertzes' possessions. John got all flustered and then said that he had forgotten to tell Tom that the urn was extremely valuable. In fact, it was a priceless and irreplaceable artifact from the ruins of Pompeii!

Amazingly, this urn not only survived the volcanic eruption of Mount Vesuvius, but also a very bumpy trip over New York City roads.

My Favorite Job

One of my first responsibilities at PCH as a young Marketing Analyst was to predict the final mailing results based on the early returns for each mailing.

This was especially important for the two largest mailings of the year, the January and July mailings. It was vital to have an early estimate as to whether these immense mailings were going to be on-plan, above-plan or below-plan. The publishers needed an early estimate in order to produce the required number of magazine subscriptions as well as for their circulation planning. And when we started to promote merchandise, these suppliers also needed an early prediction because of the huge quantity of products we sold. In addition, a good or bad January would be a predictor for the rest of the year.

In our peak years, we received approximately two million responses a day for about two weeks in a row. That's an enormous amount of mail, and it would take about two months to process it all, which is when that mailing's final result would be known. But as I have said, the magazine publishers and merchandise manufacturers couldn't afford to wait two months, so I would make my initial forecast about two weeks after the mailing arrived in the consumer's mailbox. This projection was based on the pattern of early responses and several other factors like the order to non-order ratio and order size, along with considerable intuition and judgment.

When I subsequently shifted to a management position, I taught the new Marketing Analysts how to make these projections. For the two biggest mailings of the year, however, I continued making this critical forecast for my entire thirty-year career. I was the one person the company trusted to give this forecast, and I was the first person that the President or CEO would call to predict how things looked. The whole company, in fact, waited for my prediction. The top brass didn't rely on what the Marketing Analysts projected. Nor did they have their secretaries call me to ask. They would call me themselves, eagerly asking, "What's your projection?" This happened every January and July until I retired.

As an aside, I always had some help with my January and July forecasts. Every morning when the mail arrived for our two big campaigns, I would get a call from Tom Lagan. Tom's office overlooked the front of the building where the large USPS trailers would drive up with our mail. He would watch the 18-wheel semi-trailers as they drove around the front circle, carefully observing how high the trucks would bounce as they went over the speed bumps. This would indicate to Tom how much mail was on the trucks. It would take a whole day for us to unload and approximate the number of responses received each day, but Tom could estimate what we received by how high the trailers bounced over the speed bumps. Each day he would call me as soon as the trailers arrived and give me his estimate of how much mail there was likely to be that day. Remarkably, his numbers were always right on.

Ted's First Week

This story was told to me by the highly respected Ted Kasnicki, a twenty-three year veteran of PCH and former Controller. After just a week on the job, Ted knew he was going to like working at Publishers Clearing House.

In his first week, in the summer of 1978, Ted was invited to play in the company softball game. The game was in the middle of the week and would start at 6:00 p.m. It was at its usual destination, Manorhaven Park, a local park a few miles from PCH headquarters. Everyone was welcome to join in, so the group consisted of all levels from the President on down to the clerical workers and machine operators. There were no titles once you were on the field, and we usually fielded three teams. One was called the "Teaks," the senior management team, named for their offices that were lined with teak brought back from Denmark. Then there were the "Letts," for the Lettershop department, and the "Comps," for the computer group. Other departments just filled in where necessary. The games were fun but intensely competitive, and there was occasionally a broken leg or arm as part of the ongoing competition.

After Ted's first game, John Mienik, the PCH President at the time, invited everyone back to the local pizza parlor and bar, called Andy's. This was conveniently right across the street from the park and had a large outdoor dining area for its customers. Everyone ate pizza and drank beer until about 2:30 a.m., when the festivities were finally over. Of course, John picked up the tab for everyone. Despite the lateness of the hour, we all knew we were expected, and would be, at the office bright and early the next morning.

After this long, enjoyable evening, Ted said to himself, "I think I am going to like working here!" This was just the first of many such experiences Ted would have and was quite typical at PCH. Ted went on to stay for many years, and he became an integral and respected member of the PCH family.

The following is a snapshot from that softball game in the summer of 1978.

1978 Softball Game
John Mienik/President (on the right),
Darrell Lester/Manager (at bat),
Tom Lagan/VP (center), Pete Pedersen/Manager (left)

The Trophy and the Taunt

Employees arrived at PCH one day and noticed a trophy sitting atop a ladder in the middle of the large pond in the front circle. Everyone had the same two questions – how did it get there, and what was it doing there? The trophy stayed there for two days before it was finally removed. Here is the story.

Several PCH colleagues used to play tennis on a regular basis with some of our valued suppliers. From time to time, I would fill in when they were short a player. One match was between my partner Bill Johnson (head of Human Resources at PCH) and me against Tom Lagan (a Vice President at PCH) and his partner Bill O'Brien (a print supplier). We had played a few matches previously, and Bill and I always lost. Bill and I were "B" level players and our opponents were both "A" level players.

With a match coming up in a few days, Bill and I talked strategy. How could we beat these two clearly better players? We first thought that perhaps we would take them out drinking the night before and ply them with drinks to impair their game the next night. We quickly realized this strategy wouldn't work because our opponents were both much better drinkers than we were. Bill then suggested psychological warfare. I was very skeptical but couldn't come up with a better idea, so I agreed.

Bill went out and purchased a trophy and had it engraved with *"Grudge Match Winner: Johnson/Lester."* We presented the trophy to our opponents the day before the match, telling them we were so sure that we were going to win that we had already had the trophy engraved.

The match that night was long and fierce, and a miracle did happen that evening. As underdogs, Bill and I won! That's probably why, even today, I always root for the underdog – Mets, Knicks, and Jets. I just wish one of these teams could step up to the plate as Bill and I did that night.

Bill gave the prized trophy to me, which I placed on a shelf in my office for all visitors to see. Very early the next morning, however, Tom Lagan apparently stole the trophy and had it put atop a ladder in the middle of PCH's lovely pond. Tom was looking forward to watching one of us wade through the water to retrieve our trophy. Bill and I pondered what to do, when it finally came to us. We concluded, "Let's just leave the trophy there!"

We told Tom that we had no problem with the trophy staying in the middle of the pond for everyone to see. We were more than happy to tell anyone and everyone, when asked, what the trophy was all about.

A few days later, Tom reluctantly had the trophy removed and gave it back to us. I kept the trophy on a very visible shelf in my office for many years, and when I retired from PCH, I gave it to Bill for safekeeping.

Where Am I?

This is a story shared by Tom Bass about a lost employee.

For the most part, PCH employees were smart, talented, and very able to handle a fast-paced environment. There were some rare exceptions, like the new Creative staff member who only lasted a half day before resigning due to the intense workload. Despite their ability, however, some of our employees did some dumb things at times. This was one of those times.

Our direct mail package formats were often quite complex, utilizing multiple streams of paper feeding into a press and then printing, die cutting, gluing, personalizing, and folding all in one pass. In order to have a better understanding of the production process, we encouraged our Print Buyers to visit the printing plants to view some of the more difficult formats on press. Not only did this help them attain a better technical understanding of the process, but they were also able to meet face-to-face with the production people who did our work. It was always good to put a face to the name of someone you either dealt with over the phone or who did your work behind the scenes.

Unfortunately, one drawback was that many of our printers were located in out-of-the-way places, such as Peoria, Illinois; Green Bay, Wisconsin; Newark, Ohio, etc. Often, to reach these cities, it was necessary to fly to Chicago or St. Louis first and then take a short commuter flight to reach your destination.

One day, Eileen, one of our experienced Print Buyers, was traveling to Green Bay, Wisconsin. The trip required a flight to Chicago on American Airlines and then an American Eagle commuter flight to Green Bay.

All went according to plan until she landed in Green Bay and didn't find anyone to pick her up at the airport, as arranged. After she waited ten to fifteen minutes, Eileen got tired of standing outside in the cold. Although it was April, it was cold enough that the ground was still covered with snow. Eileen went inside to find a pay phone (this was before widespread use of cell phones), and she called the printing plant and spoke to the Customer Service Representative (CSR) who handled our account and had made the pickup arrangements. The CSR confirmed that Eileen was supposed to be picked up and expressed that it was not like their driver to miss a pick up. The CSR told Eileen to call back in fifteen minutes, and that perhaps the driver was just a little late.

Eileen went back outside, looked around, and still no driver, so she went to the pay phone again and called back the CSR. Meanwhile, the CSR had received a call from the driver who said he couldn't find Eileen. You can bet the driver got an earful from the CSR, especially since Green Bay is not a big airport, and it should have been a simple matter to find someone. The limo driver was told to wait near the taxi pickup area for Eileen, as it was easier to connect at a specific location.

When Eileen called back, the CSR told her specifically what vehicle to look for and where, so there wouldn't be any more confusion. Eileen promptly went outside in search of the driver or vehicle, but again to no avail. After waiting several more minutes, she was no longer cold, but steaming with anger.

Once again she called the CSR and said neither the driver nor the vehicle was anywhere to be seen. It was right about then that Eileen realized that all the cars outside had Michigan license plates. She asked somebody what airport this was and found out she was in Grand Rapids, Michigan… 400 miles from where she was supposed to be!

Apparently, the travel agent who booked her flights had clicked the wrong city in the computer's alphabetical listing. Instead of the flight out of Chicago going to Green Bay (Wisconsin), the travel agent clicked Grand Rapids (Michigan). Both happened to be American Eagle flights. Eileen had boarded the connecting flight out of Chicago, but she went only by the flight number on her ticket, never noticing the incorrect city. When she landed, she noticed that the airport looked different than she remembered but just thought that it was perhaps remodeled since her last visit.

Eileen never made it to Green Bay and was very embarrassed. She took the jokes from her co-workers in stride when she returned to home base. She eventually was able to laugh about her misadventure.

Only One Man Could Get Away with Telling this Joke

Let me tell you a little more about my friend and respected colleague, Tom Lagan. Fortunately for Tom, he was in the right place at the right time the week PCH started in 1953... he was mowing the founder's lawn at his Port Washington home. Tom went on to work for PCH for almost fifty years.

At Publishers Clearing House, Tom was in charge of Postal Affairs, among other important production related duties, and eventually rose to the ranks of our Executive team. To the top brass at the United States Postal Service, the second largest civilian employer in the country with 656,000 members, Tom was probably the most well-known and well-liked man alive.

Tom was one of the featured speakers at a Postal Forum one day, with hundreds of local Postmasters in attendance. The USPS loved Tom and PCH, and the room was packed to hear what Tom had to say. Tom started his presentation by telling the Postal employees a joke that any other man on the planet would have been booed off the stage for telling and likely tarred and feathered on the spot. Only my esteemed co-worker, Tom Lagan, could get away with this particular joke because he was fondly thought to be "one of them" due to his extensive production background. His magnetic personality also helped him pull this off.

The joke went something like this. Two postal employees were working together, one a rookie and the other an older, long time worker. The rookie was joining the veteran for the day while he walked his postal route. They chatted throughout the day as they walked the neighborhood, delivering mail to all the homes on his route. The old pro had lots of advice to share with the inexperienced rookie. After the end of a very long day of mail deliveries, the old pro suddenly turned around and stomped on a slug. The rookie, surprised by this, asked the veteran, "Why did you do that?"

The old pro turned to him and replied, "I was tired of that damn slug following us all day!" The large audience loved it.

Another example of the expertise of my friend and colleague, Tom Lagan, occurred when he and I were on a tour of our brand new processing facility in Syosset, Long Island. One of the managers of the new facility was directing the tour, and this young manager was trying to impress us by showing how efficient they were at processing the incoming orders and non-orders. One part of the process was to stack the mail on large, seven-foot high steel cages and then wheel the cage onto an industrial scale to weigh it to get a rough estimate of how much mail was received each day. This was important because it would take several days to fully count and process each day's mail.

At this point on the tour, Tom eyed the steel cage, loaded with mail, as it was being weighed. The scale read 1,200 pounds. Upon seeing this, Tom said to the young manager, "That weight doesn't look right to me."

The manager and tour guide laughed as he replied, "No, Mr. Lagan, it's dead-on accurate."

Tom repeated that he thought the scale was incorrect, and as they rolled off the steel cage, Tom stepped right onto the scale. It showed his weight was 230 pounds. Tom then roared, "The scale is off by ten pounds."

The manager chuckled again and replied sarcastically, "That's not possible; we calibrate the scales to be exact."

Of course, this led to more banter and some heated discussion back and forth. Tom went so far as to point out that he was doing this young man's job before he was even born. At an impasse, the manager finally agreed to check the calibration.

It turned out Tom was right. All the industrial scales had been misscalibrated and had to be readjusted.

LuEsther Mertz Is Locked Out

Late in 2001, heightened security was instituted at PCH, along with all other companies in the country, due to the anthrax scare. This caused an amusing incident one day.

One weekend, LuEsther Mertz, one of the founders and General Partner at the time, came by the Port Washington headquarters with some friends who were visiting from out of town. Mrs. Mertz wanted to show off the collection of paintings that were hanging throughout the hallways of the building. The security guard looked up her name on the employee list, but because her name, LuEsther Mertz, was not there, he told her she could not enter the building.

Now if this had happened to me, I would not have been as polite as she was. I would probably have been indignant and vocal about not being let into "my building." But that was not Mrs. Mertz's style. I am told that Mrs. Mertz was very gracious about not being let in, but the very next day LuEsther Mertz was added to the employee list.

19 The PCH Bonus

Not only was the environment at Publishers Clearing House special, unique, and fun, but the company's generosity was extraordinary, as evidenced by management's annual bonuses and the financial perks for employees at all levels.

The Golf Shot

It's been over fifteen years now, and my golfing buddies still like to tease me about this funny incident involving my PCH bonus and a golf shot.

Every year over the Martin Luther King holiday weekend in January, I leave all my cares behind and go on a short golfing vacation. There are usually four of us on this weekend getaway, including my two brothers, a friend or relative, and me. We initially went to Myrtle Beach, but soon shifted farther south to ensure we had warm weather. We are not very good golfers, but one member of our group keeps track of all the scores to determine the winner at the end of four days of golf. We don't play for money but for something much more valuable… bragging rights until the next year's trip.

In 1995 we decided to go to Tampa for the first time. It was our fourth and last day of golf in the bright, warm sunshine. The usual fierce competition and bantering were in full force. I was on the 16th hole of a long par 5, stuck in a cavernous six-foot deep sand trap which sat next to a vast, undulating green. I had carefully jumped down into the sandy pit, and my fellow golfers could now barely see the top of my head. We all knew this spelled extreme trouble for me. I was not much of a player out of the sand, let alone one this deep.

As I started to take my backswing, my brother Dennis yelled out, "Hold on! I have an important phone call for you!" I had no cell phone with me and had given out Dennis's cell number in case of an emergency. I looked at Dennis, assuming he was just kidding, but he told me it was Susan Michelow, Robin Smith's personal assistant, who was calling on Robin's behalf.

I yelled back for my brother to tell Susan to hold on a moment and that I'd be right there. At this point, I was extremely worried about what this could be all about. The only possible reason I would be called while on vacation was if something terrible had happened. I took a deep breath as I proceeded to take a hurried swing out of the deep sand, my mind racing about all the possible disasters that could have happened back at PCH headquarters. Immediately after my swing, Dennis tossed me his cell phone as I was still mired in the deep sand. Not yet knowing how much damage my sand shot had caused to my score, I took the call.

As it turned out, all Susan wanted to know was how much in taxes to take out of my large annual bonus check which would be paid in a couple of days. I had already given her this information before I left for the trip, but I guess she either lost my note or wanted to double check the figure. After I hung up with her, relieved that the call was nothing serious, I climbed out of the deep trap to see where my ball was. I was prepared for a very long putt or maybe even a chip shot if I was off the green. However, my golf buddies were standing on the green, next to the flag, laughing hysterically. To me, this meant that I was probably in the sand trap on the other side of the green.

In disbelief, I saw that my ball was lying an inch from the cup. This was clearly my best shot, ever, out of a sand trap – probably because I wasn't thinking about the mechanics of my swing or about golf at all, but what I was going to hear when I took the call. They say golf is "all mental," and I guess they're right.

To this day, my golfing buddies and I still laugh about this phone call and my lucky sand shot. It's been many years, and I have yet to make a better shot from the many sand traps that I have inhabited.

Generosity

I first learned the joy of sharing from my dad's uncle, my Great Uncle Marty. The generosity of Publishers Clearing House helped as well.

PCH's philosophy was that all employees should share in the company's success. We accomplished this in several ways. First, we gave all employees an amount equal to one to two extra paychecks at year-end if results were good. This generosity took place many, many years in a row. Second, we instituted what we called "Department Awards." In this program, we gave cash awards, or bonuses, to employees who we felt deserved it based on their hard work and/or contribution. Also, as I've already mentioned, PCH doubled the retirement plan contribution for many years in a row as well. These sharing-in-the-wealth programs were very effective in getting everyone to work hard, contribute, and want PCH to do well.

In addition, for the management levels, the bonuses were extraordinarily generous, especially for the small group of Vice Presidents. The company was making so much money in the 1990's that the bonus I received during this period was an amount I never even dreamed of achieving. To make me feel better about my huge bonus in our really prosperous years, I would share the wealth with my brothers on New Year's Eve. The tradition was that my wife and I, primarily because we had two young daughters, would host a small party at our home. At some point in the evening, I would invite my two brothers to go down to the basement. I would then proceed to give them each a check for the maximum amount the government would allow as gifts. The look of amazement and appreciation on my brothers' faces was worth it all. In some years, I would be similarly generous to my wife's sister and brother. When the big bonuses stopped coming, however, I had to tell them all that the sharing was over.

The most heartwarming for me, though, was telling my hard working, blue-collar dad of my fortunate situation. He was in total and complete disbelief. He was so very proud of me, both for my accomplishments and my generosity.

Not too long after I retired, one of my teenaged daughters asked me why I didn't have to go to work anymore. It was at a time when the economy was terrible and the unemployment rate was hovering around 10%. We had friends and family out of work, and even homes in our well-off neighborhood were being foreclosed upon. My daughter was genuinely worried about our financial situation. Now, do you know how hard it is to impress your teenage children? If you're a parent, you know it's virtually impossible. But for the first time ever, I impressed my little girl. I explained to her how hard I had worked for thirty years and how successful the company was. None of that had much of an effect on her. I could tell she was still genuinely worried. Then I told her what my bonuses were in the really good years at PCH. She gave me a look of astonishment, and she said just one word, "Really?!?" I nodded yes. The broad smile on her face said it all – I had done the impossible – my little girl was impressed.

Thank you Publishers Clearing House for your generosity… to me, to all of your employees, and to those less fortunate.

20

The Best Practical Jokes

and Pranks at PCH

The story of Publishers Clearing House would not be complete without retelling some of the crazy antics of the mischievous management team. Their constant outrageous behavior contributed to the fun-loving atmosphere at PCH.

The Tell-Tale Heart

Every month we had an Executive team meeting where senior management discussed the latest company results and key issues. In attendance were all the Vice Presidents, the President, and the CEO. The meeting was always held in Conference Room B, and started promptly at 10:00 a.m. and ran until noon. At the meeting, the Finance department would present the recent mailing results and then we would turn to other important issues which needed to be discussed.

One of the attendees was Tom Owens, a very likeable and statesman-like individual, who was in charge of the Creative department for many years. Towards the end of his career at PCH, Tom's watch alarm would constantly go off and disrupt these important monthly meetings. His watch alarm was apparently set for 11:00 a.m. each day, and at every monthly meeting for two years we would all watch and wait while Tom fumbled around trying to turn off his annoying alarm. Of course, it always seemed to happen when we were in the middle of intensely debating an important issue.

At Tom's retirement party, he promised the Vice Presidents that he would be thinking about us all when the monthly 10:00 a.m. meetings came around. At the time, we didn't give much thought to his seemingly innocuous comment.

At our first monthly Executive meeting without Tom, we were all in our usual seats in Conference Room B going over the latest financial results. Midway through the meeting, at exactly 11:00 a.m., the discussion was disrupted by an annoying beeping. It sounded very much like a watch alarm, and we all stared at one another wondering whose it was.

Our first thought was that someone in the room was playing a joke, albeit not a very funny one. At exactly the same moment, we all held out our arms to show that it wasn't our watches that were beeping. We then all listened closely to try to detect where the relentless noise was coming from. For the life of us, no one could figure out where the damn "beep, beep, beep" was emanating from. But it was clearly coming from somewhere in the conference room. I remember thinking at the time, "This sound is strangely familiar."

At this point, we called Maintenance to come in to help. We hoped they could find the source of the annoying sound... and turn it off! After several minutes of investigation, our Maintenance Manager announced, "The beeping is coming from the ceiling." He then climbed on a chair, removed a ceiling tile, and there was Tom Owens' watch going, "beep, beep, beep."

Tom had apparently planted it there to remind us of him. We all thought it was hysterically funny, despite the disruption to the meeting. Tom, you got us good!

Don't Ever Bet Alan

Two very stubborn Vice Presidents made a bet, and neither would admit defeat. Tom Bass, with almost forty years at PCH, has this story to tell about their wager.

PCH had its share of Vice Presidents with strong personalities and equally strong opinions. Often these opinions and personalities clashed. On one such occasion, Tom Owens and Alan Rabinowitz had a disagreement, each feeling very strongly about his own views of a new test package. Both were very stubborn men, and they settled their disagreement by agreeing to a wager. It was a small sum of ten dollars, but each was sure he was right.

Even after the test result was in, however, Tom and Alan couldn't agree on who won the bet. Each felt he had won. Alan stated unequivocally that he was correct, but Tom claimed Alan had the terms of the bet wrong. Neither side would budge, and Alan took every opportunity to remind Tom that he had lost and owed him ten dollars, to no avail.

Soon thereafter, Tom went on vacation. When he returned, he found his office entirely cleaned out: no desk, no chairs, no file cabinets, no papers, no nothing. His entire office was completely empty, except for a phone and a small vase with a flower in it, both sitting on the floor in the middle of the large, now vacant office. Alan had had Office Services, which reported to him, empty out Tom's office to see if it would finally get Tom to pay up on his bet. Staring at his empty office, Tom immediately recognized Alan's handiwork. Tom went straight to Office Services and politely asked for his furniture and papers back. Tom, however, still wouldn't give in and tenaciously stuck to his conviction that he did not lose the bet.

At lunch time that very same day, Tom went to his usual bank to deposit his paycheck from vacation. It had been a hectic day for Tom, due to the loss of his office and all. As usual, Tom presented his payroll check and deposit ticket to the teller. The teller politely asked, "What do you want me to do with this?"

Tom replied, "Deposit it, of course."

She then replied, "I can't."

"Why not?" Tom asked with a quizzical look on his face.

The teller then handed the check back to Tom. This time, he took a close look at the paycheck, and he saw that the dollar amount read, "Nothing, nothing, nothing." He also noticed a notation in the memo part of the check. It read, "He who fucks with the master, dies without eating." Alan was also in charge of the Payroll department.

Needless to say, Tom Owens' next stop was to Alan Rabinowitz's office, where he begrudgingly handed Alan ten dollars.

The Models

I can't even begin to describe Leo Toralballa, the Director in charge of the growing Marketing Analysis department in the late 1970's. Leo had an undergraduate degree from Princeton University and a graduate degree in Mathematics from the University of Warwick in England. Leo was soft spoken, with a noticeable British accent, and had an air of aristocracy about him. Leo was known for coming to work every Friday wearing a flowing black cape and impeccably dressed for his evening at the Opera.

Leo was a speaker at one of the Direct Marketing Association's large semi-annual conventions one year. His presentation was on Statistical Modeling, and the room was packed with colleagues who wanted to hear what PCH had to say. It was highly unusual for a representative of PCH to speak at these meetings, as we were so secretive about everything we did in those days. I was there, listening from the back, and it was standing room only.

Leo started his British-accented slide presentation by showing lovely pictures of scantily clad ladies. As these pictures were flashed on the screen, a hush came over the crowd. There was soon complete silence in the jam-packed room. Leo showed about three to four slides of these voluptuous women, and then, scanning the overflowing but silenced room, he said, "Oh, I thought this lecture was on Modeling, but now I am told it's supposed to be on Statistical Modeling."

His unique sense of humor was enjoyed by all. It also got everyone to listen attentively to his technical presentation on statistical regression techniques that no one in the crowded room really understood.

You Couldn't Do This Today

Dan Doyle, a twenty-five year veteran of PCH as Treasurer, had the mindset to do whatever was necessary to help pull off a prank; he likes to tell this story.

Sam Schwartz was an older, silver-haired gentleman, and another very interesting manager at PCH. Sam was known for his loud, booming voice and extremely obnoxious nature, to everybody and everything, but especially to anyone wearing a skirt. The things that Sam said and did would get him fired in a second today. In fact, in today's office environment, he would likely have received dozens of harassment lawsuits filed against him. But back then you could get away with a lot more than you can today.

Sam's antics were known throughout the company, and everyone knew to stay out of his way. Many employees, including me, would go the long way around the building to our desks just to avoid passing through Sam's department. Underneath it all, of course, Sam was a loveable, kind-hearted man.

One day, Dan Doyle decided to play a practical joke on Sam. Dan had just finished furnishing the new Creative area where Sam's staff would reside, including Sam's new office, which had floor to ceiling windows facing a large outdoor atrium. Dan conspired with some of the folks in Sam's own department to give him the scare of his life.

Dan camouflaged his face with black stripes, put on an old infantry field jacket and army helmet, and carried an old military training rifle. Dan had been a U.S. Marine, so he had all the materials needed for this elaborate joke. A couple members of Sam's staff distracted Sam while Dan crawled furtively into the brush-filled atrium. Then Dan, in full military gear, rifle in hand, and a fierce scowl on his camouflaged face, sprung up screaming. The idea was to give Sam a flashback to his service in the Pacific. Needless to say, it scared the hell out of Sam. Dan then quickly disappeared, so Sam couldn't figure out who had done him in.

I don't suggest anyone try pulling that kind of stunt today... especially with a rifle in hand.

The Cyclops

On one of his many trips to Australia, Harold Mertz found a majestic statue that he brought back to the States, and this figure graces our main lobby. Margarete Theummler, a thirty-eight year veteran of PCH, likes to share this story about our Cyclops and a very reticent contest winner.

This story also concerns loveable, loud, brazen Sam Schwartz. One of our contest winners was at PCH headquarters one day, and her tour guides couldn't get her to smile for the pictures and video that were being taken. She apparently was just a very subdued person to begin with and totally overwhelmed by all the attention.

Sam Schwartz happened to be walking through the main lobby when they were attempting, unsuccessfully, to get our contest winner to smile. With a friendly gesture, Sam waved to our guest to say hello, and then pointed to the large infamous statue we had in the lobby to greet all our visitors. This was no ordinary statue, but an eight-foot tall, one-eyed Cyclops holding a fish. Besides its size, the most notable aspect was that our Cyclops was fully naked and anatomically correct.

Sam then walked over to the statue, put his arm around it, and loudly said to our shy visitor, "I was the model for this statue." Our guest smiled for the very first time that day!

This imposing statue is shown on the next page. I often wondered why this unusual figure was in the lobby to greet all our visitors. So I recently asked a close friend of the Mertz family. The answer I got was that Harold probably put it there because of the "mischievous little leprechaun in him."

Statue of Cyclops in the PCH Lobby
Decorated with Christmas Lights for the Holidays

How to Present a Business Plan

Steve Stark came to PCH from IBM, a much different culture from ours. He quickly learned that the conservative corporate climate he knew would not fly at PCH and soon mastered the art of the game. Steve, a ten year veteran of PCH and former Senior Vice President of Marketing, shared this story of how he adapted to the PCH antics.

Steve was presenting Marketing's Business Plan at one of our semi-annual planning meetings. In attendance at this important day long meeting was the entire senior management team, and all were listening intently to Steve as he went through his Business Plan. Steve was comfortable reviewing the plan since his lengthy document had already been scrutinized and approved by the top boss, John Mienik. When Steve finished presenting his plan, he and all the Vice Presidents looked to John for his comments. Since John had already seen the document and had approved it, Steve naturally assumed there wouldn't be much discussion.

John Mienik then got up and walked over to Steve, grabbed the Plan document, and ripped it to shreds. He then declared, "This is garbage!" Steve was shocked and dumbfounded, and he looked at John like he was an alien from outer space. There was complete silence in the room.

It was already late in the day, and John was leaving for a two-week vacation that evening, so he ordered Steve to come see him in Cambridge, New Hampshire. This was where John would be vacationing, on a farm he had just purchased. The next day, Steve flew to Albany, then drove to Cambridge, ready to work on an overhaul of the Marketing Plan, still perplexed as to what had happened.

Steve was ready for an all day work session when he arrived, and upon seeing John eagerly said, "Let's get to work."

John appeared to be in full vacation mode and with a huge grin responded, "The Business Plan is just fine – let's enjoy some time off." Apparently, this was all a set up, and all the VP's were in on it. John knew that Steve wouldn't have visited his new farm unless John tricked him into doing so.

Six months later, Steve was again presenting Marketing's Business Plan to the group. When Steve first sat down, he placed a small, fancy case on the Conference Room table. Everyone was wondering what was in the strange looking box.

As Steve started his presentation, he opened the case and took out an antique gun, which he placed on the table next to him. Steve then pointed to the gun and warned, "Just in case anyone has any comments on my Business Plan today."

The Forged Check and The Stinky Fish

This story was written by the affable, but now guarded, Sy Levy, former Chairman of March Direct Marketing, the advertising agency for PCH in our early days. You decide who got the better end of this gag.

PCH senior management didn't limit their pranks to their PCH colleagues; they also enjoyed playing jokes on our many valued suppliers. One of Alan Rabinowitz's favorite targets was his good friend Sy Levy, head of a small ad agency employed by PCH.

In the late 1970's, PCH started to run copious amounts of television advertising twice a year. The first time Sy's agency was due $1 million, Alan thought he would have some fun. Alan called Sy and insisted that our Advertising Manager, Paul Littlefield, personally bring the check to him. Sy replied that the check could just be mailed to the agency, but Alan insisted that because of its huge dollar amount, the check would be hand delivered immediately. Sy, of course, wasn't going to argue about getting a $1 million check that safely and quickly.

But in someone's haste, there must have been an oversight, because when Paul handed the check over, Sy noticed it hadn't been signed. Sy immediately called Alan, thinking it was just another one of his tricks. But Alan appeared to be very upset and insisted that Sy have Paul leave the room so Paul could privately forge our President's signature. Alan explained that he didn't want Sy to be witness to a crime. Paul did as instructed, and the matter seemingly handled, Sy and Paul went to Manhattan's elegant Shun Lee Palace to celebrate.

The two of them were enjoying a nice lunch when the maitre d' brought the house phone to their table. It was an urgent call from Alan, speaking frantically, insisting that Lou, the PCH President, objected to having his signature forged after all. Alan told Sy he would have to get the check back to him, or Alan would be fired. Sy assured Alan that he would return the check immediately, but Alan claimed he couldn't hear Sy because the restaurant was just too noisy. Sy repeated more loudly that he would return the check, but Alan repeated again that he couldn't hear him. Sy got louder and louder, saying not to worry and attracting inquisitive glances from the nearby diners. When Alan repeated yet again that he couldn't hear him, Sy screamed into the phone, "Don't worry about it! I'll take care of it!" At this point, Alan cackled wildly and roared "Gotcha!" into the phone. Sy immediately realized his intuition had been correct at the start and that it was all just a joke.

Over the years, Alan never let Sy forget his gullibility, but Sy did get even with Alan, many years later… or so he thought.

Years later, Sy invited Alan to go fishing one weekend for bluefish in Montauk. When they docked at the end of a particularly successful day, they gave away most of the fish, but Alan, in his usual insistent manner, was dead set on keeping the largest bluefish they had caught. When Alan got home, he hung up the fish in his garage for about a week in 90-degree weather. The stink must have been incredible.

After the fish had been properly seasoned, Alan wrapped and packed it up inside a very large carton and shipped it to Sy's office with very innocuous labels on it. Sy received the mysterious package, and somehow his now finely honed sense of evil warned him that this was no ordinary box; he surmised that Alan probably had a hand in it. Sy gingerly poked at the box with a letter opener, and a ghastly stench came wafting out at him. "Hmmm…. Something's fishy in the state of Denmark," Sy murmured. He immediately called his office building superintendent, gave him a few bucks, and asked him to dispose of the malodorous carton without opening it in any way.

Sy decided not to say anything to Alan and pretend the box had never arrived. This drove Alan nuts. Alan would call Sy almost every week, and Sy never even hinted that anything had happened. Finally, Alan sunk so low as to ask his lovely wife Lucille to scout around and call Sy to see if he had gotten his smelly present. Sy never gave in to Lucille either.

Alan got more frustrated every day. Did Sy get the putrid box? Did Sy open it and stink up his entire office? How could one of his practical jokes fail when it was conceived by his brilliant Mensa mind? For two years Alan dropped little hints here and there, but he never received any confirmation that Sy even knew about the box or its malodorous contents.

By now Sy was constantly on guard looking for Alan's next trap. Sy thought he won this one. However, in Sy's own words, "It came at the expense of my always being on guard, so maybe Alan won after all."

21

An Apparent Suicide
by One of Our Own

Amidst the fun, there was also some sadness.

Harry Foster was part of the PCH family for several years until he didn't make it past one of our many layoffs. Harry was a manager in one of my departments, in charge of the work we outsourced to several lettershop suppliers. When Harry got laid off in one of our many cutbacks, I was told he got back on his feet pretty quickly going to work for another firm in the direct marketing industry.

Harry was, I think, in his late thirties and had the hardy appearance of a strong, burly, well-built outdoorsman. I was told that in his younger days, in fact, he had played rugby, which is not surprising considering his imposing physical build. Harry's personality, however, did not fit his appearance at all. Harry was soft-spoken, kind, respectful, and good-natured. I never saw him angry, heard him raise his voice, or say a bad word about anyone.

I didn't know much about Harry's personal life. All I knew was that Harry was separated from his wife and had no kids. I also knew, along with everyone else, that Harry liked to drink, but that was not unusual for someone from PCH. As far as I knew, this never appeared to impair Harry's judgment or kind demeanor.

We came in to work one day and the news spread quickly throughout the building. We learned that Harry had died, and we were told that he had taken his own life. We couldn't believe the news, and many of us thought this couldn't possibly be true.

Even though Harry was no longer in our employ, he was still considered a part of our large family, and we were devastated. Whatever had brought him to his demise, we all cared for Harry and wished we could have helped him. It was an especially sad day at corporate headquarters, and it put everything else into perspective. Harry was a kind and gentle soul, and will always be remembered that way.

22

My Final Chapter at PCH

My last few months at PCH were bittersweet. I left PCH in late 2002, after we had survived "the perfect storm" – the lawsuits, the negative publicity, and white powder.

The company wasn't losing money anymore, but we weren't making any money either. Our cash reserves were completely gone, and our bottom line was right about breakeven. If one more bad thing happened to us, that would be the final nail in the coffin for Publishers Clearing House. My own personal evaluation was that it was 50-50 whether we would survive, and in private conversations with our VP of Finance and our CEO, they agreed with my assessment.

Riding into the Sunset

I finally made up my mind that it was time for me to retire. As much fun as I had over my first twenty-five years at PCH, and as much as I loved going to work every day, the last five years were another story. The constant cost-cutting, downsizing, and fighting for our lives were taking their toll on me.

Before making this life-changing decision, I spoke to a few financial advisors who agreed with my own assessment – that I could afford to retire. So then the question was – should I? I talked to some close friends, family, and my wife, to see what they thought. After much consideration, I made the decision, along with my wife, that it was time. My twin daughters were twelve, and I looked forward to spending lots of time with my family, traveling, relaxing, and playing golf.

I wasn't quite sure how to tell the top brass: Robin Smith (CEO), Andy Goldberg (President), and Debbie Holland (Senior VP). When I first informed them, my exact words were, "*Maybe it's time for me to just ride off into the sunset.*" I didn't know it at the time, but those words were going to come back in a truly haunting scene on my very last day at work.

Even though I wanted to retire, in the back of my mind, I would have liked the top executives to have at least attempted to talk me out of it. But I knew my colleagues all too well and knew they wouldn't. I knew that Andy and Robin would consider my early retirement as just another cost-cutting measure. I didn't blame them for that, but even so, I was saddened by this. However, I had spent a lifetime in those halls, and I was ready to retire. At the time, I remorsefully thought to myself that when I leave, the last bit of heart and soul will be leaving PCH. In the years since I left my second family, this same thought has been expressed to me by several former business colleagues, which is certainly heartening to me.

In my discussions with the top executives, we agreed that I would take six months to transfer my responsibilities, contact the numerous outside suppliers with whom I worked, and tie up loose ends. I decided that my very last day at the office would be December 20, 2002. This was extraordinarily hard for me as I genuinely felt that PCH was my second home, but I knew it was my time, even though I was only fifty-one.

Two People I Owe

In addition to the generosity of Publishers Clearing House and to Alan Rabinowitz's insight in hiring that naïve twenty-one year old kid, I owe my early retirement to two special people. The first is to my Uncle Rudy, an extraordinary man. The second is Ted Kasnicki, a PCH colleague and friend, and the most financially savvy person I know.

UNCLE RUDY: My family and I were very close to my Uncle Rudy and his family. He was the first one from his generation to go to college, and he earned his CPA with the help of the GI bill in 1951. However, he wasn't happy just being an accountant. His dream was to become a doctor, but that was not possible for him. He needed to support himself and his family, and he couldn't get that degree while working during the day. So instead, while working full-time, he went to Brooklyn Law School at night and in 1954 earned a law degree. With his education and degrees as both an accountant and a lawyer, Uncle Rudy had a very successful career, and he worked hard to support his family.

Uncle Rudy was the first person to take my brothers and me golfing. We were in our twenties at the time. How my uncle, a 10-handicap golfer, had the patience for our utter incompetence and complete lack of golf etiquette, I will never know. We thought that golf was a silly game at first, but then we came to love it.

While in his late fifties, my uncle decided he would finally ease towards retirement. He bought a condo in an incredibly lovely community called Boca West in southern Florida. This was a large, luxurious resort community nestled on 1400 acres of paradise, overlooking four lush golf courses. His plan was to take the next year or so to wind down his business affairs and then to enjoy the good life. Sadly, my uncle never spent a day fully retired in his beautiful Boca West home. He passed away unexpectedly on June 1, 1985, at the young age of fifty-nine after a very brief illness. This whole situation taught me that, if you can, retire early.

TED KASNICKI: Ted was the Controller at PCH for many years. I often tell Ted, whenever I see him, how much his advice helped me.

It was April 2000, and I had just received my PCH quarterly retirement account statement. The stock market had been down recently, and I was concerned because of the large amount in my nest egg. I happened to be in the men's room, with Ted in the next stall, the day we received this quarterly statement. Ted and I chatted about how we both had about the same amount in the company's retirement plan, and how our nest eggs were getting to be quite substantial. I asked Ted what he thought I should invest this large sum in. Without hesitation, he said to me, "When you reach a certain amount, like we have, put it in something safe like Treasuries." The very next day I shifted all of my retirement funds out of the stock market and into a safe investment getting a paltry 4% to 5% interest per year. At the time, that rate was considered very low, but it was safe. Shortly thereafter, the stock market nosedived and went down 40%. Every time I see Ted, I thank him for his timely advice. Without it, I could never have retired early.

Two Good-Bye Parties

My first good-bye party was a formal lunch with Robin Smith and all the Vice Presidents at one of our favorite local restaurants. Andy Goldberg, who had recently been made President, presented me with some very humorous trinkets from our Merchandise department. As we all laughed, I thought to myself... I was the last of a breed at PCH, the last of the senior management team who was taught by the eccentric but lovable original PCH Vice Presidents. My luncheon comrades and I shared some much-loved PCH stories, and everyone wished me well.

The second farewell celebration occurred about a week later at a local upscale restaurant and bar, but we only made use of the large bar space. It was an informal get-together that some of my staff had arranged, and I had no idea who would be attending. As it turned out, people from many departments as well as former employees and outside suppliers came to wish me farewell and join in the festivities.

As I was cleaning out my office that was filled with a lifetime of "stuff," I came across some items that I put aside, intending to give them to some of my friends at this celebration. For one, I found a golf ball with "Oh Shit!" printed in bold letters on it. I don't even recall where I got this, but it was the perfect gift for my friend Michael Brennan, a PCH supplier with whom I enjoy playing golf. Michael is notorious for hitting the ball very, very long, but generally way to the right – and he is often heard cursing (with those exact words) after he sees where his ball is headed.

I also had a wooden sign carved with the word, "Attitude," which sat on my desk for many years; it was the first thing a staff member or visitor would see while sitting across from me. About two weeks before I left, one of my employees thought it would be a good idea to permanently "borrow" my beloved sign because she knew I would be retiring soon. The afternoon of the party, unbeknownst to her, I sneaked into her office and retrieved the sign. I then carefully wrapped it up and presented it to her at the celebration. Needless to say, we shared a good laugh over this.

I hadn't spoken to my old friend Bill Johnson in a while (he was no longer working at PCH), and I hoped he would attend my final celebration. Just in case, I had wrapped the tennis trophy he and I had won years earlier. Bill surprised me by showing up, and I ceremoniously presented the trophy to him, telling him it was now his turn to safeguard our prize. The picture of me presenting Bill Johnson the trophy is shown below.

Farewell Party
Darrell Lester presenting our tennis trophy to Bill Johnson

The Most Extraordinary and Heartwarming Good-Bye You Could Imagine

I spent over half my life at Publishers Clearing House. I have many great memories and made many life-long friends. As you can imagine, my last

204 ⇔ *Darrell Lester*

day was bittersweet. I was looking forward to my new life in retirement but was sad because I was leaving the family I had known for thirty years.

Taking my very last drive out of the back parking lot to the front of the building, around our tranquil pond, I saw the totally unexpected. Apparently, one of my departments had been waiting for me to leave, and there were about a dozen of my staff standing outside by the front entranceway. They seemed to be shuffling around, and then they formed a straight line, standing arm in arm. Each one was holding one or two very large and visible three foot letters. With the letters arranged, my colleagues spelled out:

"We will truly miss you!"

Their farewell touched me. I waved to them all as I slowly drove my car around the PCH pond for the very last time. At that moment the sun was just setting – and it was the most brilliant sunset I had ever seen. I stopped the car and stared in awe at the sky. I couldn't believe it. I was literally *"riding off into the sunset"*... exactly as I had told the top brass several months earlier.

It was a haunting departure. I thought to myself that my Uncle Rudy and my mom and dad were smiling down at me. That sunset, forever a picture in my mind, I will never ever forget.

23   Life in Retirement

After thirty years of working long hours at Publishers Clearing House, I really had no idea what life in retirement would be like. But in my first week, I knew there was something I had to do. I had to visit my dad at the cemetery.

My dad passed away several years earlier, and I hadn't been to the cemetery in a while. I wanted to tell him that I had retired and let him know that it was okay. My dad was always extraordinarily conservative with his finances, working hard his whole life in order to send his three sons to college. An example of his frugality was his discomfort any time one of his sons bought a new car. He would disapprovingly ask us, "Why did you have to buy new?" I knew the visit to the cemetery would be very emotional, but it was something I felt I needed to do. My wife joined me. At the graveside, with tears flowing, I said out loud, "I'm retired, Dad, and I know I'm still young, but don't worry... I can afford it." I think he understood.

In my first year in retirement, it just so happened that one of my brothers and a good friend were both between jobs for most of the year. We spent a lot of time hanging out together; we took in some matinees, played racquetball and golf, and just enjoyed each other's company doing guy stuff. So my first year, having two good buddies around made the transition to life in retirement much easier for me.

With all my newly found free time, I decided to borrow an idea from the Prize Patrol. I started what I coined the "Surprise Patrol." I initiated several trips, surprising a few old friends whom I hadn't seen in many years, as well as some good friends who don't live locally. These unannounced visits have been so much fun that now some of my friends have started doing the same to me. Even my daughters have gotten into the act.

Besides the Surprise Patrol, about two years after I left PCH, in September 2004, I put together a PCH alumni reunion party at my home. This was for former PCH employees only, no current employees allowed. About fifty to sixty former colleagues came, and they came from all over, including one living as far away as Puerto Vallarta, Mexico. Attendees ranged from former secretaries to a former President and everything in between. There were recent alumni and old-timers alike, and the closeness that we had achieved while working at PCH had not faded. There was genuine joy on the faces of co-workers who hadn't seen each other in many years. Below is a snapshot of me with beloved former President Lou Kislik. Lou is on the right.

But life in retirement has not been all joyful. Around my second year of retirement, something occurred that I hadn't planned on nor expected. My young sister-in-law was afflicted with early-onset Alzheimer's, and I spent every day for an entire year helping her and her family. This was very difficult, but I knew my help was desperately needed, and I was glad I could be there for my brother and his family in their time of need. My sister-in-law has since passed away.

My First Visit Back to Port Washington

About a year after I left PCH, I made my very first trip back to the small town of Port Washington where PCH headquarters is located. It was a work day for most, and I was having lunch with my oldest friend, Allan Lomnitzer, who lives in town.

I found myself feeling very anxious about this visit, wondering who I might run into from PCH. I thought to myself, "What good friend and former colleague would I see?" Would I run into Andy Goldberg, the current President and CEO, my highly respected rival at PCH? Or perhaps Todd Sloane, current Senior VP, the creative genius at PCH with whom I had had many private and enjoyable conversations? Or maybe Dave Sayer, the seasoned head of the Prize Patrol who resided in the teak office next to mine? Or perhaps it would be Debbie Holland, current Executive VP, the remarkably talented youngster that I grew up with at PCH? Or maybe one of my former staff members who still worked there, whom I dearly missed.

My friend and I finished lunch, and it looked like I was not going to run into any of my former PCH family. I found myself extremely depressed over this as I was hoping to see at least one former colleague.

I left the restaurant completely dejected and started to cross Main Street, heading towards my car. But just as I was about to get in, I heard a car horn blasting. The honking, getting louder and louder, was coming directly towards me. As I looked up, I saw the PCH garbage truck. The driver was madly honking his horn and waving to get my attention. He stopped the white truck with the PCH logo right in the middle of Main Street, holding up traffic. We talked for a quick minute, and then he went on his way.

I was absolutely elated! Although it wasn't anyone from the senior management crowd (Robin, Debbie, Andy, or Bill) or the Prize Patrol

(Dave or Todd) or any of my old staff (Karen, Steve, or Michael), I was still thrilled to have run into a friend from PCH. I consider everyone at PCH a part of my second family.

Publishers Clearing House Today

I am very happy to report that PCH is still around today. They are the sole survivor of the multi-magazine sweepstakes agencies. Many new multi-magazine agencies are around nowadays, but these companies sell only via the Internet (none use direct mail), and the number of subscriptions sold are nominal. The list includes Magazines.com, MagazineYellowPages.com, ValueMags.com, and Amazon.com, to name just a few.

With respect to the use of sweepstakes or contests today, its use is prevalent in the Internet world, as well as in retail and other consumer related industries – but is virtually absent in the direct mail industry. In fact, these days, the only sweepstakes you'll find in your mailbox is from Publishers Clearing House.

The bad news for the publishing industry, and to the consternation of hundreds of magazine publishers, is that PCH has shifted their product mix and now sells mostly merchandise, with only about 10% to 15% of their sales coming from magazines. The Prize Patrol, however, still gives away all that money to surprised winners around the country... and they still make a couple of lucky consumers rich every year.

With respect to how PCH is doing today, I would speculate the following. The 50% decline in results we realized in the difficult years was due half to the negative publicity and half to the softening of our sweepstakes language. Since the negative publicity is gone, that part of the negative influence is also gone. This is consistent with what I have heard, and I have also heard that PCH is back to being profitable. But the size of the business is small and the number of employees is modest at about 400, many of whom work in the Internet division. Sadly, it's not the company it was when I grew up there. I wish all my business colleagues who are still there all the very best.

PCH is still privately held and the company is largely owned by the charitable foundations established by the Mertz family. Harold and

LuEsther Mertz are gone, and they have no surviving children: their son Peter Mertz passed away in 1954 in a Swarthmore College fraternity hazing accident, daughter Joyce Mertz left us in 1974, and Richard Mertz, Harold's stepson from his second marriage, passed away in 2001. The philanthropic spirit of the Mertzes, however, lives on with over half of the company's profits now going to benefit charitable causes. The largest single owner is the LuEsther T. Mertz Charitable Trust, while smaller pieces are owned by other charitable trusts established by the Mertz family, and by heirs of the deceased founders.

I was surprised when I recently heard about some additional legal trouble for PCH after ten years of no news on this front. Apparently, an investigation by some of the states raised concerns that PCH was not fully complying with the prior agreement and that consumers could be confused by the nature and language of some of the company's promotional mailings. I don't know much more about this than what I have read in the news. In September 2010, the media reported that PCH signed a new supplemental agreement with thirty-two states and the District of Columbia that includes stronger provisions than the prior agreement. Plus, as part of the agreement, PCH was required to pay $3.5 million to the states.

As for the town of Port Washington, the legacy of Publishers Clearing House will live on forever. In a fitting tribute to LuEsther Mertz, the street next to the Post Office was renamed "LuEsther Mertz Plaza." In the local newspaper, *The Port Washington News*, a recent article described PCH's legacy as follows:

"Ask anyone living in Port Washington and environs if they have ever known someone who worked at Publishers Clearing House and you will get a resounding, 'Sure!' or 'My mother worked there,' or 'I worked there every summer through college,' or 'My neighbor was a manager there,' or 'Who hasn't worked there?!'"

The local paper summed it all up by stating, "Over its 50 years in town, Publishers Clearing House has hired thousands of residents on a regular or part-time basis, and the company has become a famous and respected part of this centuries-old community jutting into Long Island Sound."

Acknowledgments

Writing this story has been an especially fulfilling task, and a lot of fun at the same time. But I could not have done it without help from my family, friends, and business colleagues.

I would like to recognize three of my mentors at PCH: Alan Rabinowitz, Bruce Pantano, and Jeannie Clarke. The lessons you taught me were invaluable, along with your friendship.

To the management team still remaining at PCH (Andy, Debbie, Todd, Bill, and Robin): I would like to say from the bottom of my heart, I wish you smooth sailing and the wind at your back.

To my former staff that still remains at PCH: I miss you all terribly and cherish our time together and our camaraderie. You made my thirty years at PCH nothing short of wonderful.

To my PCH alumni friends: There are so many of you who made my time at PCH incredibly enjoyable. I also greatly appreciate your contributions to the PCH story. I hope I did justice to the tale of Publishers Clearing House. I would be remiss if I didn't give special recognition to a few of my closest business colleagues and friends, all of whom encouraged and helped me with this engrossing project. Thank you Tom Mastrocola, Bill Johnson, Tom Lagan, Tom Bass, Steve Juhasz, Lori Bertucelli, Bert Rowley, Ted Kasnicki, Lou Kislik, and Hank Rossi.

To my literary advisors, David Yale and Seth Soffian: Thank you for your valuable feedback and guidance. And a very special thanks to Dr. Roni, my wife's sister, for your great editing prowess and wisdom. You enabled me to capture the true spirit and character of a remarkable and unique company and important part of my life.

To Dennis, Rich, Big Al, Dan, and Jay: A big thank you for all your help, advice, and encouragement on this once-in-a-lifetime project.

To Alex Amoling, a gifted up-and-coming filmmaker friend of my daughter and recent graduate from Emerson College: Your alluring simulation of PCH's towel-clad contest winner was perfect for the cover of my book.

And last but certainly not least is to my wife, Rocey, and my daughters: You were my inspiration for writing this book. I hope you enjoy hearing about the corporate side of my life at an extraordinary company. And a special acknowledgement to my wife for your unending patience, support, and help over the three years it took me to write this story. I couldn't have done it without you.

CPSIA information can be obtained at www.ICGtesting.com
Printed in the USA
BVOW072123210512

290622BV00002B/19/P